THE

SEX

★ ★ ★ FACTOR

KATE JOHNSON

THE SEX FACTOR

The Essential Teen Guide

PICCADILLY PRESS • LONDON

First published as *Sex – How? Why? What?* © 1994
This edition revised and updated © 2012
by Piccadilly Press Ltd,
5 Castle Road, London NW1 8PR
www.piccadillypress.co.uk

Text copyright © Kate Johnson, 2012

The right of Kate Johnson to be identified as Author of this work
has been asserted by her in accordance with the
Copyright, Designs and Patents Act, 1988

A catalogue record for this book is available
from the British Library

ISBN: 978 1 84812 200 0 (paperback)

1 3 5 7 9 10 8 6 4 2

Contents

Introduction

Sex is a very natural thing. After all, humans are born with all the body bits they need to have sex, and most people get the urge to use them at some point in their lives – whether it's to make a baby, to show their love for someone, or just because it feels fabulous.

We're pretty sexual creatures right from the minute we're born. Even babies touch their private parts because it feels nice, and if you think about it, little kids' games like doctors and nurses often involve a fair bit of crafty groping. Once you hit your teenage years, sex is likely to be in your thoughts one heck of a lot. The point is that sexual stuff comes naturally to us, and there's nothing wrong with enjoying your own body – it's as normal a part of being a living creature as eating, sleeping and going to the toilet.

Back in the days when we all lived in caves, playing with yourself or having sex were probably about as much of a big deal as those other bodily functions. Several thousand years on, however, sex has become a more complicated issue. The mere fact that this book exists proves the point – after all, when did you last see a book about how to go to the toilet? Or hear politicians arguing about what age kids should start being taught the ins and outs of sleeping?

Sex is no longer just a bodily function, but a really big deal. It all comes down to centuries of changing attitudes about sex and our bodies, not to mention the fact that these days we have all sorts of things to worry about – like unintended pregnancies and sexually transmitted infections. This means that we often have a load of questions and worries and sometimes feelings of embarrassment and confusion about sexual things too. This can make it hard to know where to go to ask our questions and put our minds at rest.

Hopefully, reading this book will be a big step towards becoming as well-informed about every aspect of sex as possible. In it, you'll find all you need to know about how your body works, how the opposite sex's bodies work, contraception, sexually transmitted infections, pregnancy, problems with sex and, of course, loads of information on the act of love-making itself – that all-important Sex Factor! You'll also find the answers to lots and lots of questions. Most of us fret about the same things (which is quite reassuring in itself, isn't it?), so hopefully some of the questions will be the very same ones that have popped into your head and got you wondering, or might pop into your head in the future.

Learning all about sex will be a big step towards making your own sexual experiences (when and if you're ready to have them) informed, safe and unconfusing – not to mention wonderful, heavenly and fun! Sadly, no book can claim to unravel the mysteries of love and find you the perfect partner. Even the best books on relationships can't *promise* to make anyone's personal life go smoothly.

Nope, dealing with the love part is *your* job. Of course, you don't have to be in love to have sex, but remember that true love and good sex are two of the greatest pleasures on the planet. Experiencing both at the same time is about as near perfect as life can get.

Part 1

ALL ABOUT YOU

The first part of the book is all about *you*, as you sail into the exciting, uncharted territory of puberty, towards adulthood! Hopefully, it will help you get to know your changing body and feelings, as well as thinking about attitudes to sex – yours and other people's. Bon voyage!

Chapter 1

Your Body

When you're a little kid, you don't really give your body that much thought. Then along comes puberty and – bang! – that great, relaxed attitude you had goes right out the window. It's bye-bye to peace of mind and hello to hours of wondering, worrying and wiggling yourself into odd positions in front of the mirror to get a better look. In this chapter we're focusing on:

- Getting to Know Your Body
- Puberty – What's the Deal?
- Periods
- Help! Your Puberty Questions Answered
- When You're Really Worried

Puberty

Puberty is the proper word for the time in your life when your body changes from a kid's body into an adult's. It's a funny-sounding word, but puberty itself isn't very funny at all. Weird – yes, surprising – yes, scary – sometimes. Embarrassing? Wonderful? Horrible? Exciting? Yes, puberty is indeed all these things and much, much more. But funny? Sadly not. With light relief in such short supply, puberty can be a tricky time. The best way to cope is to take it easy and keep on top of what's going on by being smart, aware and totally well informed. And what better place to start getting clued-up than right here?

Getting to Know your Body

OK, so you know that boys' and girls' bodies are pretty different right from the word go. Let's check out exactly who's got what, and where.

Boys' Bodies

If you're a boy, you're probably already well acquainted with your main bit of apparatus – the penis. *Willy, cock, knob, dick, prick, tool* and *tackle* are just a few of the weird and wonderful nicknames for it. Your penis is made of soft body tissue, chock full of blood vessels. When you get sexually excited, blood rushes into the vessels, and a ring of muscles at the base of the penis tightens to stop the blood flowing out again. The result is that your penis gets bigger and harder and can stand up all by itself. This is called getting an *erection* – or in slang terms, a *hard-on* or *boner*.

Taking a closer look, your penis is made up of two sections: the *shaft* (the long bit) and the *head* or *glans* (the bobbly bit on top). You might also hear the glans called a *helmet, bell end* or *knob end*. It contains a greater concentration of nerve endings than are usually found in your body, which is why it feels extra nice when you touch it. The glans is usually covered and protected by a moveable bit of skin called a *foreskin,* although you might have had yours removed for religious or medical reasons. This is called being *circumcised.*

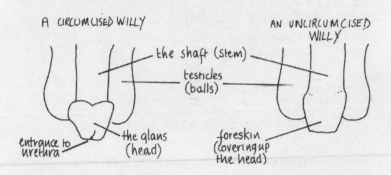

A CIRCUMCISED WILLY

AN UNCIRCUMCISED WILLY

the shaft (stem)

testicles (balls)

entrance to urethra

the glans (head)

foreskin (covering up the head)

Underneath your penis are your *testicles* or *testes* (also called *balls, bollocks* and *nuts).* These two small round organs are held inside a kind of skin bag, called the *scrotal sac* or *scrotum,* and they store *sperm* – the tiny living cells which have the potential to make a baby. When you're warm and relaxed, the scrotum looks soft and you can clearly see the shape of the balls inside. When you're tense, sexually excited or just a bit chilly, the whole thing gets much firmer and pulls itself up closer to your body in a neat, crinkly-looking little package.

There's lots going on inside your body, too. The little hole at the end of your penis is the entrance to a tube called the *urethra* which does two jobs. Firstly, it leads from your bladder and lets your wee out. Secondly, it joins up with the tube which comes from two internal sex organs – the *prostrate gland* and the *seminal vesicle*. These two organs produce and store *seminal fluid*. Seminal fluid is a sticky, whitish liquid which gets mixed up with the sperm to make *semen* (also known as *spunk, cum, jism* and *juice*).

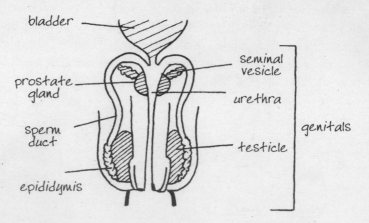

When you play with yourself, have sex or even have a sexy dream, and you reach a point where you can't get any more sexually excited, you have an *orgasm* – a great, big, lovely, rushing feeling of excitement, and that's when *ejaculation* happens. This means that a batch of the sperm and semen you've been storing up comes spurting out of the end of your penis. This is also known as *coming* or *climaxing*.

All of a boy's most important sexual equipment is below his belt. It's worth noting, however, that you've also got two nipples. Unlike a girl's nipples (which work as outlets for milk when she has a baby), yours don't serve any particular function. They *do* have a bunch of nerve endings in them, though. This means that it can feel good when they're touched, and you might notice that they go hard if you squeeze, rub or stroke them. In fact, you will probably enjoy being touched and stroked on many different parts of your body.

AN ERECT WILLY

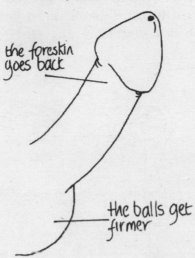

the foreskin
goes back

the balls get
firmer

Girls' Bodies

Unlike a boy, a girl has most of her important bits tucked away inside her. Your *vagina* is a passage which starts with an opening between your legs and ends about nine centimetres up, at the entrance to your womb, which is called the *cervix*. There aren't as many nicknames for vaginas as there are for penises, but there are still quite a few, like *fanny, hole, quim, snatch* or *pussy*.

Your vagina is a very versatile thing: it stretches to let a penis in during sex, lets your periods out, and is also the route that your babies will take from your womb to the outside world, if you decide to have any. If you have a closer look between your legs, you might find that the entrance is covered by a thin film of skin called a *hymen* (see *Losing Your Virginity* on page 76).

Inside, you've also got two *ovaries*, where your body stores eggs (which have the potential to make babies), and two

7

tunnels called *Fallopian tubes* for the eggs to travel down when they're ripe. Once a month an egg settles in the lining of your *uterus*, or womb. This egg will either be fertilised by a sperm, or be expelled from your body through your vagina (see *Periods* on page 13).

A GIRL'S INTERNAL BITS

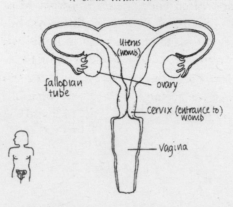

There's plenty going on outside your body too. Firstly, there's what's called the *mound of Venus* – the soft bump of flesh over your pubic bone, where your pubic hair grows. Moving down-under, everything is more hidden away, but if you take a close look (using a hand-held mirror helps!), you'll find that on either side of the entrance to your vagina are a pair of little lips (called the *labia minora*), and a pair of bigger, outer lips (the *labia majora*). Directly above all that is a tiny little hole which is the entrance to your *urethra* – the tube that leads from your bladder. This is where your wee comes out. Right at the top of all this equipment is a delicate little bump, protected by a tiny hood of skin. This is your *clitoris* (some people call it *clit* for short), a neat bundle of nerve endings.

The clitoris is a very interesting and important bit of you, because its only reason for being there is to make you feel nice, sexually, when it gets touched.

Although your clitoris feels and looks just like a little bump, about the size of a very, very small pea, it's actually a bit like a tiny penis, made up of a *shaft* and a *head*. Like a penis, blood rushes into it when you get sexually excited, making it go hard – though you wouldn't necessarily notice this happening. When your clitoris is touched, the excitement builds up, and often ends with an *orgasm*. Most girls don't release liquid (ejaculate) at orgasm, like boys, but a few may find that they do – and the amount of liquid will vary from very little to quite a lot. This liquid is thought to come from the urethra (wee-hole) but it is not urine. One thing's for sure – whether you ejaculate or not, an orgasm is a really wonderful feeling! (See Chapter 2 for more info.)

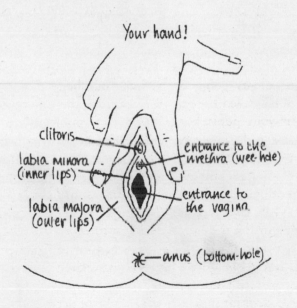

Your hand!

clitoris

labia minora (inner lips)

labia majora (outer lips)

entrance to the urethra (wee-hole)

entrance to the vagina

anus (bottom-hole)

Moving higher up your body, you'll find your *breasts* – also called *bosoms, boobs, tits, knockers* and about a million other names. If you haven't gone through puberty yet, you'll just find your nipples. Inside, behind them, are all sorts of milk-making glands so that you can breastfeed your baby if you want to. They're also there to give you sexual pleasure, thanks to lots of sensitive nerve endings, especially in the nipples. And, like boys, you will probably find that you enjoy being stroked and touched on many different parts of your body – not just your private parts!

Puberty – What's the Deal?

Throughout this book, you're bound to notice that we keep coming back to one particular fact: everyone is different. The puberty situation is no exception – everyone hits puberty at different times. For boys, we're looking at some point between the ages of ten and sixteen. For girls, it's between nine and fifteen. Everyone's puberty follows a different pattern, too – the changes can happen really fast and all at once, or pretty slowly, spaced out over a number of years. Whatever, most people find that their puberty is all over and done with by the time they're seventeen (girls) or eighteen (boys). If you started early, you could finish much earlier. Having said that, some changes can go on happening right up until your mid-twenties – for instance, boys' bodies and faces can continue to get hairier, and girls' breasts can get bigger.

Despite the differences in *when* puberty happens, *what* happens is much the same for everyone. Here's what you can expect:

Boys
• Your penis and testicles will get slightly bigger.

• You'll get hard-ons more often, sometimes when you'd least expect it!

• You might experience *wet dreams* – having an exciting, sexy dream, then waking up to find that you've come in your sleep. (These are called *nocturnal emissions*.) You may not remember the dream or the orgasm, but you'll probably notice a damp patch on your night-clothes or on the bed, where you ejaculated.

• You'll grow extra body-hair, especially under your armpits and near your tackle. The hair above and around your penis and balls is called *pubic hair* (aka pubes), and it's usually darker, coarser and curlier than the hair you've got elsewhere. You might also get hair on your chest – although some men never do.

• Your skin may get greasier, so you'll be more prone to getting spots than before.

• Your hair might get greasier and need washing more often.

• You'll sweat more, especially under your armpits, and you may notice that your sweat smells stronger than it used to. Although fresh sweat smells fine, stale sweat doesn't, so if you don't wash regularly and use a deodorant, you'll get pretty stinky!

• You'll get taller, often in a quick growth spurt.

• You'll put on weight. This doesn't mean you'll get fat – just that your body will fill out into a more adult shape.

• You'll get stronger.

• Your voice will 'break'. This means that eventually it'll be deeper and lower – a man's voice rather than a boy's. Some boys simply wake up one morning to find they've got a new voice, but for others the change can be slower and weirder – you could go through a period where your voice wobbles alarmingly between being high and low, with the odd mysterious squeak and croak coming out now and then!

• You'll get hair growing on your face – and unless you want a beard or a moustache, you may need to start shaving.

Girls

• Your nipples will grow bigger and maybe get a little darker.

• You'll grow breasts. They might start off feeling like lumps. You might notice a tingly feeling or even 'growing pains' as they develop, and find that they suddenly become very sensitive – accidentally getting elbowed in the boob at this stage can make you see stars!

•The little lips on either side of your vagina get fuller, but you probably won't notice the change.

• You'll discover the odd bit of white gooey stuff in your pants. This is called *discharge*, it comes out of your vagina, and it's just a sign that everything inside is working properly.

• You'll grow pubic hair above and around your private parts, which will probably be darker, coarser and curlier than hair you've got elsewhere.

• You'll grow hair under your armpits.

• The hair on your legs will get slightly darker and thicker – and therefore more noticeable.

• You might get the odd hair (or a whole bunch) growing where you didn't expect it – such as around your nipples, on your tummy or even on your face, around your chin or upper-lip.

• Your skin might get greasier, so you'll be more prone to getting spots than before.

• Your hair might get greasier and need washing more often.

• Your armpits will sweat more and smell stronger, so you'll need to wash daily and perhaps use a deodorant to keep yourself smelling sweet.

• Your body will probably fill out into a more womanly shape, with curvier hips and a more pronounced waist. You are likely to put on weight as this happens.

• You'll get stronger.

• Your voice will get a bit lower and deeper, but you probably won't notice it happening.

• You'll start having periods . . .

Periods

Here's the low-down:

• The medical term for periods is *menstruation*. Slang terms amongst others include *coming on, time of the month* and *having the painters in*.

• This is what happens when you get a period: one of your ovaries releases a ripe egg (this is called *ovulation*). The egg travels down the Fallopian tube towards your womb. Your womb makes a special, thick lining just in case the egg meets a sperm, gets fertilised by it, and needs a safe, comfortable place for a baby to grow. If the egg doesn't meet any sperm, your body knows that there isn't going to be a baby, so it gets rid of the lining, along with the egg and a bit of blood.

• You'll know for sure when you get your first period because you'll find blood in your pants. It can be bright red, like the blood that comes out when you cut yourself, but it could also look dark red or brown. You can't see the egg or the womb-lining or anything like that – it all just looks like ordinary blood.

• A period normally lasts anything from two days to a week.

• Some girls bleed quite a lot, others don't bleed much at all.

• Women usually have their periods regularly, about once a month, but when you first start getting them, the chances are that they'll be very irregular and you probably won't have any idea when your next one is due.

• When you've got your period, you'll need to use something to catch the flow of blood. You can choose between *sanitary towels* and *tampons*.

Sanitary towels

Sanitary towels are long, flat, soft pads with a sticky strip underneath to fix them inside your pants. They catch and absorb your blood. You can buy towels in pharmacies and supermarkets, and there's often such a huge choice of brands, absorbencies, thicknesses and shapes that it can seem quite confusing. Most people try a few types until they find a favourite. The only guideline to follow is that if you bleed a lot, it's best to pick a towel that is extra thick or extra absorbent (sometimes called 'super'). Others have 'wings' – little sticky side-flaps that you stick underneath the gusset of your knickers. These are pretty good because they stop the towel from bunching up when you move around, so there's no chance of blood staining your pants.

The advantage of towels is that they're simple to use, health-risk-free, and you know for sure when they need changing.

The disadvantages are that some people think they feel 'bulky' and they can sometimes show through tight clothes. If they're not changed often enough they may smell a little, and you can't go swimming in one. They are not always easy to dispose of away from home – never flush them down the toilet, as they cause pollution in waterways and seas.

Tampons

A tampon is a short, fat stick of cotton wool with a string at one end for pulling it out. It fits snugly inside your vagina and absorbs the blood before it can come out. You can buy tampons from all the same shops that sell towels, and again, there's lots of choice. The two basic types are those with an *applicator* (made of plastic or cardboard that helps you push the tampon inside you) and those without (which you just push in with your finger). It's worth trying both so that you can find out which you prefer. Tampons also come in different thicknesses. This doesn't mean their actual size, but how much blood they can absorb. If you have very heavy periods, go for a 'super' tampon, otherwise 'regular' is fine. Many brands also have a type called 'slender' or 'mini', which are slimmer, easier to put in, and especially good for younger girls.

All tampons come with very good, detailed instructions of how to put them in, and once you've got the hang of it, it only takes a second. Never worry about 'losing' a tampon inside you – it's impossible! If you have trouble getting one out (like if the string goes inside you) you can always gently reach inside your vagina with your thumb and forefinger and try to pull it out that way. If you're having no luck and panicking, your doctor can do it for you – they're used to it.

The advantage of tampons is that they're totally hidden, even if you wear tight clothes, and once they're in, you can't feel them at all. The downside is that you can give yourself an infection if your fingers aren't clean when you push one in (without an applicator) or take it out. There is also a small risk of getting a very nasty, serious infection called *Toxic Shock Syndrome,* especially if you accidentally leave a tampon in for too long (we're talking days here, not hours). The leaflets in boxes of tampons explain it all in detail, but the main thing to remember is that if you throw up or feel sick, get a high temperature, feel faint, pass out or get a body-rash while you're using tampons, you must take the tampon out, call your doctor or go to a hospital immediately. If you get any of these symptoms in between periods, you should always check for a forgotten tampon and get medical help if you find one. If left untreated, TSS can kill you.

You should always change a tampon every few hours. If you're scatty and you think you might forget, you might be better off using towels.

Even if you prefer tampons, it's a good idea to switch to sanitary towels at night.

Period Pains and Premenstrual Syndrome (PMS)

Some people don't feel any discomfort at all when they get their periods, some just feel the odd strange, pulling sensation low in their tummies, while others get terrible 'period pains' – nasty low-down stomach cramps. You can also get backache, feel sick, get dizzy and even get a bit sweaty and feverish. If your period pains or other symptoms are really bad, the best thing to do is lie down with a hot water bottle on your tum or back until you feel better, although some people find that going for a walk or getting some other kind of exercise can help just as much. Other things that help: a long, hot bath; massaging your back and stomach; eating dark green, leafy vegetables and nuts which contain magnesium and calcium – good for calming womb muscles.

You can buy painkillers such as Feminax especially for period cramps, but ordinary painkillers work for most people. If your pains are really bad, see your doctor, as there are various medications you can get on prescription.

It's nice to know that you won't necessarily have painful periods for the rest of your life – many women find that things get much better as they get older.

• Some people find that they get grumpy, tearful, tired or

depressed, and can feel 'bloated' a couple of days *before* their period comes. This is called *premenstrual syndrome,* and it's no fun. Sometimes just knowing *why* you're feeling so bad can help you to cope, but if you find it unbearable, it's worth chatting with your doctor, who might be able to help out. Many women swear by a natural remedy called Evening Primrose Oil, which is available in capsules from supermarkets, chemists and health-food shops. As with period pain, gentle exercise and a good diet which avoids coffee, soft drinks and chocolate can help too.

• Period pains and PMS are no joke. If you feel like you need to stay home, or just take things a bit easier than normal, you have every right.

• As long as you feel OK, your period shouldn't interfere with your life at all – it's fine to do *everything* you'd normally do. There are lots of myths about things you should avoid during your period – such as swimming, having sex, washing your hair or having a bath. Ignore them. These myths aren't just silly, they're downright unhelpful. In fact, swimming can be great for relieving period cramps, and bathing (or showering or just washing) is *essential,* otherwise all that blood is going to go stale, and you'll end up pretty stinky downstairs – not a good thing.

Help!
Your Puberty Questions Answered

Almost everyone finds *something* that worries them about their bodies during puberty. Here's just a handful of the most common concerns.

Boys

*My penis looks normal until it gets hard. Then it has a bend in it.
Is there something wrong?*
No – penises come in many shapes. There are probably as
many around with a bend as there are straight ones, and they
all work exactly the same.

*My balls appear to be different sizes and one hangs down lower
than the other. Am I normal?*
Totally. No one has a perfectly matching pair of testicles, and
no one's testicles hang exactly side-by-side.

Can you break your penis?
Not exactly, because it doesn't have a bone inside it to break.
Nevertheless, it's still important to be careful with your penis
when it's hard, because it can get damaged – and be *very*
painful – if it gets violently squished or bashed at an angle.

*I'm a bit worried. If the tube inside my penis can let out both wee
and spunk, how does my body know which one to let out at the
right time?*
It just does, so don't panic about accidentally weeing inside
your partner during sex or ejaculating in a public toilet when
you were just planning on having a wee. Both the wee-tube
and the semen-tube have tiny gates at the end of them, and
only one can be open at a time. Your body always makes sure
it's the right one.

*Being circumcised never bothered me until I told some friends
who weren't. They told me that it means my penis is smaller, I
can't wank and that I won't be able to enjoy sex. Are they right?*
No way. Circumcision doesn't affect the length or width of
your penis – in fact, when a willy is hard, it's darn near

impossible to tell the difference between one with a foreskin and one without. Moreover, you can enjoy masturbation and sex just as much as someone who isn't circumcised. There are even a few *advantages* to not having a foreskin. It's been medically proven that if you are circumcised you are less likely to get infections in your reproductive organs or bladder. Plus, you won't have the problem of bodily secretions collecting under your foreskin to create a slightly smelly white mass. The word for this gunk is *smegma,* but it's often known in slang terms as *cock-cheese.*

However, this doesn't mean that circumcised boys can get away with not washing their penises.

I think my penis is abnormally small. I've seen other people's and they've all been loads bigger.

On average most penises are about the same size. For the record, that's between five and eight centimetres when they're soft, and about fifteen when they're stiff. Sure, some people are going to have bigger ones, and – yes – some are going to have smaller ones, but it's unlikely that yours is as preposterously tiny as you think. Bear in mind that when you see other people's penises you're seeing them from a different angle. You're looking *across* at theirs, and *down* at your own, which is going to make yours seem a bit smaller, and everyone else's a bit larger – it's an optical illusion. Remember too that your tackle compresses and tucks itself closer to your body when you're feeling jumpy, tense or cold – so if you've been doing your comparisons in communal changing-rooms or showers, you've probably started with that disadvantage anyway! Even if your penis really is smaller, bear in mind that it could still grow some more if you haven't yet finished going through puberty. Most of all, though, remember that size really *isn't* important.

But don't girls prefer big penises to small ones?
Actually, if a girl hasn't had many sexual experiences, she's likely to find sex much more comfortable (and therefore more enjoyable) if her partner has a slightly smaller one. Generally, most girls and women would agree that penis size doesn't have a lot to do with how much they enjoy sex. There is a saying that goes, 'It's not the size, it's what you do with it that counts'. This is true, and it's also not just what you do with your *penis* that counts either: it's what you do with your hands, your mouth, your whole body and just the way you behave. If you're thoughtful, affectionate and sexy in bed, it really doesn't matter if you've got a dick like a crayon or a giant salami. It's also important to remember that girls get a great deal of their nicest sexual feelings not in their vaginas (where your penis goes) but in their clitorises which you touch with your hands, mouth or groin – not your penis.

I saw a thing on the internet about surgery that can make your penis bigger. I've also heard about creams and machines you can buy that do the same thing. Does any of this stuff really work?
Medical professionals agree that there is no cream or contraption that can make your penis permanently bigger, although that doesn't stop some dodgy manufacturers from making products that claim to. At best, the rubbish they sell is just a waste of time and money. At worst, you could end up damaging your equipment – so steer clear. Surgery for penis enlargement does indeed exist. It's a very expensive procedure which involves snipping a tendon at the base of your penis, and although it leaves you slightly bigger, many people who have had it have done complain that their sex lives have got *worse,* because their willy goes flopping all over the place, and they can't control it. You've also got to remember that having a general anaesthetic can be risky, and that *any* surgery is painful, can leave you scarred, and carries big risks of infection and

human error. That's why it's never worth having surgery you don't really need. Learn to love your penis and respect yourself, and don't let the money-grabbing people who invent these fads take advantage of your insecurities.

I get erections a lot for no particular reason, when I'm least expecting it. It's a nightmare at school, because people make fun of me. Help!

If it's any comfort, rest assured that you're perfectly normal, and it won't go on forever. Some boys find that if they can get a chance to masturbate (and come) before school, it keeps their penis nice and quiet for the rest of the day! Otherwise, it's just a question of minimising the embarrassment. As soon as you realise you've got a hard-on, find an excuse to sit down (with your hands over your lap!) until it goes. If you can't sit down, put your hands in your pockets and stretch the fabric right out. You could also try thinking about something boring and totally unsexy (like homework, chores, the bus timetable, smelly socks) – it might help speed the unwanted erection on its way.

It's a shame your classmates are so insensitive and stupid. Still, when everyone else hits puberty, it's bound to happen more often, and to other people, and the joke will wear thin eventually. Whatever, neither the teasing nor the erections will go on forever – so hang on in there!

I reckon I've been through just about every change in puberty but I've never had a wet dream. Does this mean my penis is not working properly?

Your penis is fine – not everyone has wet dreams. It could be that you *are* having wet dreams, though, and just haven't noticed, perhaps because you're having them early and the damp patch has dried before you wake up.

Oh my God I think I'm growing breasts! Am I turning into a girl?
No. You're just experiencing a common, harmless but rather
annoying condition which happens to a lot of boys in puberty.
Little pads of extra fat grow behind one or both nipples, stay a
while, then disappear. There's nothing wrong with you, you're
no less 'manly' than the next guy, and your 'boobs' will go
away eventually. It's really no big deal in the great scheme of
things, even though it's probably very embarrassing and
horrible right now. Sadly, there's not much you can do apart
from getting a nice selection of baggy tops and waiting,
although you may want to visit the doctor, too, just to put
your mind at rest.

*My dad hasn't got any hair on his chest, and I'm not showing any
signs of getting any either. Meanwhile, my mate has grown lots,
and I feel a bit wimpy next to him, and worry that girls won't like
me once I get my top off.*
If you suspect that your dad's lack of hair has been passed down
to you, you're probably right. Having a smooth chest certainly
doesn't make you any 'wimpier' than anyone else, and as to
which looks better – it's just a matter of taste. Remember that if
a girl likes you enough to get into a 'top-off' situation, then she's
not going to be put off by what's under your togs, even if she
prefers hairy chests to smooth ones.

*Looking at the posters that my sisters pin up on their walls, I've
noticed that most famous men and male models have smooth
chests. It looks like I'm going to be pretty hairy, and I'm a bit
worried that it'll put girls off.*
Yes, lots of famous men have smooth chests, but lots don't.
Sometimes it can be hard to tell exactly what people have,
because lots of men wax their chests to get the smooth look. It
could just be in fashion right now, but in a few years' time
they'll probably all be frantically sticking on chest-wigs! The

bottom line is that fashions really aren't worth worrying about. Although some girls might prefer smooth to hairy, or hairy to smooth, most really don't give a monkey's about what's on your chest – if they fancy you, they're going to fancy you regardless.

I'm growing quite a lot of facial hair, and I want to start shaving. What do I need?
Firstly, a razor of some sort – either a disposable safety razor or one you can change the blades on (which you use to shave when your face is wet), or an electric shaver (which you use dry). If you want to wet-shave, you could get some shaving foam, too. You can use lather from a bar of soap instead, but some guys find it makes their skin go a bit dry and flaky. What you really *don't* need is aftershave – it serves no real purpose, it stings, and it can irritate and dry your skin. If your skin gets blotchy or itchy after shaving, you might want to use some sort of moisturiser or soothing shaving balm afterwards, instead.

Girls

Is there any way to tell when you're going to start your periods?
Not really, although most girls start at around the same age as their mothers did, or slightly earlier. You could also keep a lookout for discharge (a white stain in your pants). It's usually a sign that all your internal bits are kicking into gear, so if you have it regularly, the chances are that your periods will start within the next year or so.

I have discharge, but it's not white, and it smells funny. Is this normal?
Normal discharge can be off-white, but it shouldn't smell of anything in particular when it comes out. If you are a little

itchy downstairs as well, you might have a vaginal infection, or an NSGI (non-specific genital infection). This isn't anything terrible, but a trip to the doctor could be in order to help clear it up. There's no need to be embarrassed about vaginal infections – everyone gets one at some point, and you don't necessarily get them from having sex (although smelly, itchy discharge can be a sign of some sexually-transmitted infections too – see Chapter 6 for more details).

Would I be right in thinking that if I haven't started my periods, I'm not releasing eggs yet, so I can't get pregnant if I have sex?
No, no, no! You *can* get pregnant without ever having had a period. Think about it: you release your first ripe egg a couple of weeks *before* your first period, and if you have sex around that time, you could easily get pregnant. You won't have the foggiest idea about when you're going to release your first egg, so you'll need to take as much care as someone who is already having periods.

Can girls have wet dreams?
Sex researchers reckon that you can indeed have an orgasm while you're asleep and dreaming. Chances are, though, that you wouldn't know it, as girls don't usually leave the obvious physical evidence that boys do – ie, a wet patch on the bed.

I think there's something wrong with me because my nipples go inwards instead of sticking out . . .
You have what's called inverted nipples, and there's nothing wrong with you at all – lots of people have them. They may stay inverted all your life, or change when you get older. Either way, they're not a problem and they won't make any difference to your enjoyment of sex or your ability to breastfeed a baby.

I feel like a freak because one of my boobs is bigger than the other.
Everybody has one bigger than other, and the chances are that you're the only person that has noticed yours because you've spent ages studying them! If the size difference is really enormous, rest assured that they'll probably even up a bit more before they finish growing.

How do I know when I need a bra?
If your breasts feel uncomfortable when you run or play sports, you could definitely do with a bra. Otherwise, it's entirely up to you whether you want to wear one or not: if you just fancy wearing one, treat yourself; if you hate the idea, don't bother. It's true that if you wear a bra every day, as soon as your breasts have grown (regardless of their size) they won't get droopy so quickly as you get older. However, everyone's bosoms drop eventually – they would even if you wore a bra twenty-four hours a day from the minute you were born – so it's nothing to worry about. Besides, there's nothing wrong with droopy boobs – many women actually find that they *prefer* the shape of theirs when they get a bit lower, rounder, fuller and softer.

I'm sixteen and my breasts haven't changed size for two years. Is that it, then?
Not necessarily. Bosoms are one part of you (or two parts!) that change shape throughout your life. You could get another growth spurt later on in your teens, or even in your early twenties. The size and shape of your breasts can also be affected by putting on or losing weight, going on the pill, getting pregnant, breastfeeding or just getting older.

My boobs are small. I wish they were bigger . . .
Why? All breasts feel equally nice when they're touched, and size makes no difference to breastfeeding. Little bosoms are

just as feminine, attractive and sexy as big ones. Both have been in and out of fashion so many times that it's not worth even thinking about. If you're worried about boys' attitudes, sure – some prefer big ones, but an equal amount prefer small ones. Most just like breasts, full stop, and are more interested in what they're attached to, anyway. Any intelligent, nice guy isn't going to be swayed one way or another by the contents of your bra. Stop beating yourself up and learn to love yourself the way you are.

A friend told me that going on the pill can make your boobs grow. Is it true?
Some girls find that being on the pill makes their breasts grow, due to the big dose of hormones, but it's not all that common. Most girls experience no change in breast size at all, and others find that it makes them put on weight all over. It's definitely not worth going on the pill just because you want bigger boobs. For more about the pill – and its side-effects – check out Chapter 5.

What about cosmetic surgery to make your boobs bigger?
Getting breast implants is not something you should rush into. We're talking about a serious surgical procedure under general anaesthetic (ie, you get put to sleep). Your bosoms are cut open and plastic bags containing either saline (sterile saltwater) or, more usually, silicone (a kind of squishy plastic) are put in before you get sewn back up again. Afterwards, you're bandaged up and it can take weeks or months for all your bruises and pain to go away. Like all operations, breast-enlargement carries risks. You could be left with permanent scars, your chest-muscles can get hard and lumpy around the bags and the bags can leak or burst inside you, which can be extremely dangerous.

The surgery is expensive (implants aren't available on the

NHS unless you've lost a breast through disease or in an accident), and surgeons will not operate on a girl until her breasts have reached their full adult size. Even if all goes swimmingly, remember that your new, big bosoms will actually be big, fake lumps of plastic that don't look or feel 100% real.

If you are truly desperate for bigger boobs, buy a padded bra, or stuff a pair of socks or some tissues in a regular bra – it's cheap, effective, risk-free, and easily reversed if you feel like going back to your original size.

My boobs are too big! I wish they were smaller . . .
As with people who feel that their bosoms are too small, the best thing you can do is try to learn to love yourself the way you are, and try not worry about it too much. Be proud of your wonderful bosoms! Buy a good, supporting bra for comfort and try to avoid the temptation to hunch over or slouch – it won't hide your breasts, and could cause you horrible problems with your back.

What about breast-reduction surgery?
Yes, you can have an operation to make your bosoms smaller. Like any operation, there are a few risks involved, but it's generally simpler and safer than having your breasts made bigger. It's still expensive, but if the NHS reckons that your case is worthy, it *is* possible to get it done for free. To qualify, you'd need to have *very* large boobs and be able to prove that they were horribly uncomfortable, stopped you from enjoying everyday activities, made you feel terribly depressed, and perhaps gave you problems with bad-posture and back pains. You would need to have a doctor's report, so the first step would be to have a chat with your GP.

I'm not keen on all this new body hair. What's the best way of dealing with it?

You don't *have* to get rid of body hair – millions of women choose not to. If you want to, though, there are lots of different ways. Like:

• Shaving – easy and cheap (all you need is a disposable razor or one that you change the blades in like a Ladyshave and some soap lather). Good for leg and armpit hairs, and OK for your 'bikini-line' (ie, the pubic hair that shows when you wear knickers or a swimsuit). The hair grows back in a few days, and feels a bit bristlier than before.

• Depilatory cream – cream that dissolves leg and armpit hair. (You can also get a gentler kind for your bikini-line.) It's easy to use, and hairs grow back more slowly and less bristly than if you'd shaved.

• Waxing – putting a special wax on your legs, armpits or bikini-line, then ripping it off – with all your hairs in it. Ouch! You can buy ready-waxed strips, or have it done by a beautician (which can be costly). Hair grows back slowly, though (it takes a couple of weeks), and feels soft, because it's brand new hair.

• Electric epilators – little electric gadgets that you run over your legs, catch the hairs and pull them out from the root. This has all the benefits of waxing, only it's easier, and cheaper in the long run (once you've bought the gadget, that's it for life).

All these products should be available from pharmacies and (apart from the epilator) large supermarkets.

I've grown some hairs on my face, and I'm not happy. What can I do?

You can pluck them out with tweezers, use facial depilatory creams or waxing kits or, if you're fair skinned, lighten the hairs with a special facial bleach to make them less noticeable.

There's also electrolysis – a simple procedure done by a qualified beautician, where the hairs get zapped at the root by a little electric beam and hopefully stay away for good. However, you need a course of treatments, and it's not cheap – think carefully.

Warning: if you have a hair growing from a mole, snip it off with scissors. Never pluck or wax it – moles are sensitive things that are best left alone.

What about hair around the nipples or tummy?
Follow all the same rules as for facial hair.

Can I use deodorant between my legs?
Nooo! Don't even try it! You're talking about a *really* sensitive area that could easily get irritated, and besides, you don't *need* deodorant down there. Just a regular wash every day, with unscented soap, will keep everything healthy and fragrant.

When You're Really Worried

As you can see, most of the stuff that worries us is perfectly normal and not really worth fretting about. However, if something's worrying you a lot, and you just can't get it out of your mind, or you really feel that something might be wrong with you, it's always worth a visit to your doctor. It's a sad fact that many people avoid visiting their GP, for all sorts of reasons. You might be embarrassed about your problem, and wonder how the doctor will react. You might feel that if there *is* something wrong, you don't really want to know about it, or that if there isn't, the doctor might be cross with you for wasting his or her time. You should never let these – or any other – fears put you off visiting the doctor. If a problem is worrying you, it's always worth checking out, just to put your mind at rest. That's what doctors are there for. Gather up your courage, and just remember:

• Doctors have seen everything before, so they're not likely to find anything surprising, disgusting or funny – they're very matter-of-fact.

• A doctor will never laugh at you, tell you you're being silly, deliberately embarrass you or tell you off (for time-wasting or anything else).

• If it turns out that you *do* have a problem, it's always better to know about it. Almost every problem can be sorted out, and you'll feel so much better knowing that it's being dealt with and that you don't have to worry any more.

• If it turns out that you *don't* have a problem, you'll be able to forget all about it and get on with your life without wasting all that energy on worrying.

• Doctors get paid for seeing patients – that's their job. Every day, they'll be visited by some people with serious problems, some people with simple problems, and some who turn out to have no problem at all. A doctor will be used to seeing all of them.

Chapter 2

The New You

It's not just your body that changes during puberty. The way you feel changes too, and that can be even more confusing. Suddenly you're experiencing emotions you've never had before, thinking new thoughts, worrying about new problems. Sometimes it can feel like you're changing so much, and so quickly, that you hardly know yourself any more. This chapter should help you understand the new you a little better! In it we look at:

- Sexual Feelings
- Gay, Straight or Bisexual?
- Masturbation

Getting to know the new you

Probably long before you even consider having sex, you'll find yourself thinking and wondering about it, asking yourself more and more questions. You'll discover all sorts of things about what kinds of people you fancy and what excites you, and perhaps you'll get to know your own body better sexually by *masturbating* – touching your private parts because it feels nice.

What's really going on is that you're turning into the person you're going to be for the rest of your life – the adult you, the new you. Getting to know the new you is just like getting to know someone else – interesting, complicated and sometimes surprising. It's a huge task that's partly a wonderful, thrilling adventure and partly a huge, confusing pain. But it's one of the most important things you'll ever do, because the more you understand and feel comfortable with yourself, the easier it'll be to help other people to get to know you, and know what you want out of a relationship. And that's the key to having a fantastic, happy and secure love-life in the future.

Sexual Feelings

Just as everyone frets over whether their bodies are 'normal', we all wonder if what's going on in our heads is what's supposed to be going on. Here are some very common worries . . .

I think about sex all the time. Am I normal?
You bet! You see, the hormones that cause all the physical changes in your body during puberty don't just make you

sprout hairs and suchlike. They also get working on your brain, and bingo – you've got urges like you've never felt before. Quite apart from this, sex is dead interesting, and thinking about it can be a very nice, exciting thing to do with your spare time! Even if you know that you're perfectly healthy and normal, thinking about sex all the time can still make you feel uneasy, because you can feel that you're losing control of your brain.

It happens like this: at first you find you think about sex a bit, and it's fine. Then it starts popping into your head of its own accord. You don't mind that either, and nor do you care much when it starts distracting you in dull moments – after all, it's far more interesting and fun to think about sex than, say, maths homework. But time goes on and you suddenly realise you're even thinking about sex at times when you would have been thinking about stuff you *liked* – such as who's going to win Saturday's football match, what happened on *EastEnders* last night, whether you can beat your brother's hi-score on *Halo*.

It can feel like sex is invading your life, changing the way you are – or thought you were – as a person, and it's a scary feeling. Just as you can't stop the changes taking place in your body, you can't stop what's happening in your head. It's still your brain, but right now it's like a computer trying to process all sorts of complicated new software that's been dumped onto its hard-drive in the middle of a huge power-surge. It's going to take a little bit of time before everything gets sorted and you can go back to using it for whatever you want, but it *will* happen. By all means, look around for other new interests you can throw yourself into for distraction. Otherwise, just try to relax and carry on with your life.

I'm not interested in sex at all. Is there something wrong with me?
Not at all. There are a hundred degrees of 'normal', and

while it's perfectly healthy to have your brain teeming with sexy thoughts, it's equally healthy – and equally common – not to have the slightest tad of interest whatsoever. If sex is the furthest thing from your mind, it could be because your hormones haven't kicked in yet, or it could be that they have, but you're not affected as strongly as the next person. Equally, it could be that you've got a busy life with so many other interests that you just haven't got the time and energy to spare for thinking about sex. In any case, the chances are that a day will come when sex plays a bigger part in your thoughts and your life, one way or another.

Certainly there are some people who never get very interested in sex, and make a conscious choice that sex is not going to be a part of their life. These people are usually happy and confident about their decision. If the thought that you might never want sex makes you panic or feel sad, then it's very unlikely that you'll turn out that way. The mere fact that you're worrying shows that sex *is* important to you, and it's likely that your natural urges will hit you in the future.

I often imagine having sex with people I know, or famous people. I really enjoy it. Is it OK?
This is called *fantasising*. It's more than okay, and nearly everybody does it at some time in their life. It's just like daydreaming, only its main purpose is to make you feel excited in a sexual way.

A fantasy can be about anyone and anything. It can be a quick thought that pops into your head for a moment, or a long, detailed story that goes on for ages in your imagination. In other words, thinking for a second what it might be like to snog your teacher is a fantasy, and so is spending twenty minutes imagining passionate sex with all the members of your favourite pop group in a big bath full of melted chocolate.

Some people fantasise just for fun, others like to do it

while they masturbate, and find that it makes them feel even more excited than if they were just touching themselves. In fact, many people find that what goes on in their heads can excite them just as much as what's going on down below. Many, many people also fantasise while they're having sex (see Chapter 7).

Fantasising is a fantastically healthy way to discover more about your own sexual feelings, so you should never feel guilty about doing it.

If you fantasise about something, does it mean that you really want it to happen?
No way. Once people get into fantasising, they often find their thoughts getting wilder and wilder and involving people or activities that they definitely wouldn't want to get involved with in real life. It's a very common, very healthy thing – it means you're exploring the boundaries of your imagination and finding out what excites you.

People are often surprised by what excites them in a fantasy, and can even find themselves getting turned on by an idea that would normally horrify them. When this happens, you can feel pretty disgusted at yourself and wonder how you could even have *thought* of such a thing, let alone got excited. If you find it totally impossible to shake off your guilty feelings about a particular fantasy, it's obviously better to give it a rest than be miserable. Generally, though, you should never beat yourself up about what goes on in your head. Remember that you're healthy and normal, and that a fantasy never hurt anyone.

So any fantasy is fine? Even a really weird one?
Sure. And the chances are that your 'weird' fantasy has already been thought of by a trillion other people. Here are just a few popular fantasies: having sex with parents, with brothers or

sisters, with close friends, with strangers, with people you don't even like; having sex with lots of people at the same time; having sex with an animal, or being licked by one; watching other people have sex; having others watch you while you have sex, do a striptease or play with yourself; being paid to have sex; visiting a prostitute; being tied up or forced to have sex or doing it to someone else.

The only time you should worry about your fantasies is if they are very violent, and get more violent. If you get turned on thinking about injuring or killing animals or people, you might have a problem, and you need to talk to a professional counsellor or therapist as soon as possible. See under *Counselling* in Resources and Contacts at the back of the book for ideas on finding a counsellor locally.

I'm having a lot of rude dreams. What's up?
You might have guessed it – sexual dreams are yet another trick that your hormones are playing on your brain. Not to mention the fact that if sex is in your thoughts more often these days, then it's bound to be in your dreams too.

Dreams are often harder to cope with than fantasies because you can't control what you dream about. You can find that you're having sexy dreams about all sorts of people and situations that you wouldn't touch with a barge pole but, as with fantasies, it doesn't mean that deep down you want these things to happen – it's just your imagination doing a bit of exploring all by itself! It can be weird, but try not to let it bug you too much. Sometimes a sexual dream can stay in your head all day, and facing someone you've dreamt about can be embarrassing. Just remember, though, that no one can tell you've had a rude dream, so there's nothing to worry about!

I've fancied people in the past but now there's one person I can't stop thinking about and I feel like I'm going crazy. What's going on? Is this love?

Sort of. It's actually what's called a *crush* or *infatuation,* and it's another mental side-effect of all this growing up your body is doing. It's like a little test-run for all the complicated emotions you're about to start feeling. What's the difference between love and a crush? In very simple terms, love is what happens when you get to know someone really well and are having a relationship with them. A crush is a feeling you get about someone you're not having a relationship with – like a teacher, a famous person, a friend or someone you see regularly but don't know that well. You might fantasise about going out with that person, kissing them, having sex with them, living with them or even marrying them!

You'd think that a crush wouldn't feel as intense as love, but actually it can be equally exciting, confusing and exhausting – if not more so, because it's all going on in your head, instead of in real life, and you're not getting any feed-back.

Crushes can be wonderful – your heart leaps when you see the object of your desire, just talking about them or thinking about them makes you happy, you feel warm and bursting with passion.

Crushes can also be hideous – you feel desperate to be with that person, miserable, lonely and frustrated because you're not or can't be, and despairing because you can't imagine you'll ever feel the same way about anyone else. Everyone who has ever had a crush experiences both the good *and* the bad side, and, unfortunately, there's very little you could do to 'get rid of' a crush. Luckily, though, crushes don't last forever. You *will* find someone else you feel strongly about, and with any luck they'll feel the same way about you and it'll be a million times nicer – honest!

Straight, Gay or Bisexual?

Research shows that 90-98% of the population fancy people of the opposite sex. They're called *heterosexual, hetero,* or *straight.* The other 2-10% are sexually attracted to people of their own sex. They're called *homosexual,* or *gay,* and if they're female, they can also be called *lesbian.* There are also plenty of slang words like *homo, bender, poof, bum-boy, lezzie* or *lezzer, dyke* or *queer* and other ruder, more jokey names, too – usually describing sexual things that gay people might get up to. All these are pretty insulting, and anyone with half a brain wouldn't use them, although dyke and queer are often used by gay people themselves.

Many people are attracted to *both* sexes. The word for this is *bisexual* (pronounced 'bye'-sexual), or *bi* for short.

Being gay or bi shouldn't make your life any more complicated than anyone else's, but unfortunately it can and often does, largely because of other people's attitudes and hang-ups. Although, thankfully, it is much easier to be openly gay or lesbian than it used to be, many homosexuals still face discrimination in some situations and sometimes risk verbal and physical abuse. Wondering if you might be gay shouldn't be a traumatic thing, but these sad facts mean that it often is. Still, just trying to make sense of your *own* feelings, never mind those of prejudiced people, can be puzzling enough . . .

I've only ever had serious crushes on people who are the same sex as me. Does this mean I'm gay?
The way you feel now is not *necessarily* the way you'll feel for the rest of your life. Many girls and boys find that they have crushes on people of *both* sexes as they grow up, then end up being straight. Even people who *only* fancy people of the same sex and have sexual experiences with them while they're young

sometimes wind up being straight later. Having said this, the idea that same-sex crushes and relationships are 'just a phase you're going through' can be unfair. A lot of people discover very young that they are gay, never doubt it and never change. It's also worth remembering that a lot of gay adults went through their teens having only heterosexual feelings, and discovered their true feelings later – so being straight when you're young could fairly be described as 'just a phase' too!

For now, do yourself a favour and try to resist the temptation to 'label' yourself as any one thing or another. Remember that when you're attracted to someone, it's hopefully not just about what's between their legs. Perhaps you *won't* ever find you fancy anyone of the opposite sex, and will decide one day that you are definitely gay, but for now you certainly don't have to pin yourself down and put yourself in a pigeonhole if you don't want to.

The world would surely be a much easier place to live in if we stopped making a big deal about our differences, and looked at our similarities instead. After all, we're all just *people* who get attracted to other *people,* and what sex anyone is should be no more important than what colour hair they have.

I've got a crush on my teacher, who is the same sex as me. Apart from that, I only fancy people of the opposite sex. Does this mean I'm bisexual?

Maybe, but again, don't worry too much about it – you've got plenty of time to find out. Many psychologists believe that *everyone* is bisexual, whether or not we choose to do anything about it. A huge amount of straight adults will have had a crush on someone of the same gender.

Crushes aren't always sexual, anyway. You can feel very passionate about someone because you admire them, think they are attractive and clever, and wish you could be just like them. You usually get this kind of crush on a teacher, prefect or other older person, and it doesn't necessarily mean that you want to have sex with them.

I'm pretty sure I'm gay. Should I tell my friends?
Telling people that you're gay is sometimes called *coming out,* and there's no 'should' about it. If you want to share your feelings with them, then do. If you don't, then you've got every right not to. It's a hard decision to make, because you don't know how they're going to react. It's a sad fact that people are often very uptight and uneasy about things they can't understand, and also that there are still people out there, young and old, who are *homophobic* – that is, anti-gay. If you can make your friends understand you, you've won half the battle. You might need to remind them that you're still exactly the same person, and even though you may be different to them in one way, life is not all about sex, and you still have all the same things in common as you had before.

Friends of the same sex may also wonder if you fancy *them* and feel funny. Yes, it's stupid, and it's their problem, but it's still a good idea to make it clear that you don't.

If your friends tease or reject you, they're not worth hanging on to anyway. You have been very brave to come out, and deserve to be surrounded by friends, old and new, who love and value you for who are you – sexuality and all.

I think I might be gay, but I'm very confused. I'd love to have someone to talk to about my feelings, but I don't know who would understand.
When you're trying to get to grips with anything at all, the best person to talk to is someone who has been in the same situation themselves. If you don't know anyone who is openly gay, don't worry – there is an excellent helpline run by the London Lesbian and Gay Switchboard on 0300 330 0630. (Please note that they're a nationwide service – not just for

Londoners!) This line is staffed by gay and bisexual people who are also trained counsellors, and will be understanding, helpful and very easy to talk to.

How can you tell if someone is gay?
You can't. There are plenty of myths about what gay people look like or how they behave – ie, gay men are feminine, dress oddly, talk in 'camp' voices like Graham Norton, and walk around wiggling their bums; lesbians are 'butch' and wear men's clothes, huge boots, have very short haircuts and talk in fierce growly voices. These are just silly stereotypes, and very few gay people actually fit them. Most look, talk and dress exactly the same as the next person – because apart from who they choose to go to bed with (which is really nobody else's business), they *are* the same.

Masturbation

You might well have heard about masturbating before. Some people call it *wanking* and *jerking* or *tossing off.*

Masturbating basically means touching or rubbing your private parts to give yourself pleasure, and often – but not always – an orgasm.

These are some of the many things that people want to know about masturbating.

What's an orgasm?
An orgasm, also known as *coming* or *climaxing,* is what happens when you've reached the highest point of sexual excitement. It sounds like a really big deal – and it can feel like one too – but it's surprisingly easy to make happen.

Here's how it goes: you'll find that when you touch your

penis or clitoris in certain ways, it feels nice. If you carry on doing whatever it was that felt nice, you'll find it starts feeling better and better, and that's when you start to get a feeling that *something* is going to happen. It's a little bit like when you know for sure that you're going to sneeze. When you've become as physically excited as you can possibly get, that's when it happens – a really big, ultra-lovely feeling that happens in your genitals, but sends waves through your whole body.

After you've had an orgasm, you feel a huge sense of release that is very satisfying – again, a bit like sneezing, only a million times more enjoyable. It's quite hard to imagine what having an orgasm is like until you've actually had one, but once you have, you understand your body better and will always find it quite easy to recognise when you're about to come in the future.

Is masturbating normal?
Very, very normal. Almost as normal as eating, sleeping and using the loo. Some people never masturbate, and are perfectly happy not to, but most men and women do it at some time or another, and many people of all ages do it regularly and often. Small children often discover that it feels nice to touch their genitals, or to rub them up against things, but then get interested in other activities, and forget all about it for a while. Most people rediscover the joys of playing with themselves around the time when they hit puberty, and spend the next few years doing it a great deal. Once you hit adulthood, you'll probably do it a bit less often, but many people carry on doing it for the rest of their lives.

Is it harmful?
Far from it. It can actually be quite useful, because it teaches you to understand how your body works, and what feels nice

for you, sexually. Knowing what turns you on can help you when you are ready to make love with a partner. Plus, many people find it's a good way to release tension and help them get to sleep!

So it's not harmful at all? But I heard . . .
Yeah, yeah, there are a million rumours about what terrible things masturbation can do to you. Perhaps you've been told that it makes you go blind, or become short-sighted. Or that it stops you from ever being able to make babies, rots your brain cells, sends you insane, damages your genitals, makes them shrink, ruins your chances of having a normal sex-life or gives you some other nasty medical ailment or disease. Boys are also sometimes told that it 'uses up' all their sperm. This is all total and utter rubbish. There has never been any medical evidence linking masturbation with infertility, mental health or any other illness or problem, and as the average sexually mature male produces many millions of new sperms every day, it would be impossible for him to run out! There is not a bit of truth in these, or any other rumours about masturbation being bad for you.

How did the rumours start, then?
They were invented by adults many years ago who disapproved of masturbation for any number of reasons, as a way of putting people off masturbating. Some people disapproved because they felt that sex was 'dirty' and that it was 'wrong' to feel sexual pleasure. Others had strong religious beliefs that sex and the sexual organs only existed in order for married people to make babies, and that using the genitals for any kind of sexual pleasure – especially outside of marriage – was 'sinful'. There are still people about who think the same way. Of course, everyone is entitled to their own beliefs, but people also have a right to know the truth.

Facts are facts, and the plain truth is that masturbation is not harmful.

So how do you do it?
There's no particular way to masturbate – everyone does it a little bit differently. Nevertheless, here are the basics:
• Boys usually do it by gripping their penis and sliding their hand up and down in a jerky motion that gets gradually faster. Boys who have a foreskin often slide it up and down over the head of their penis.

This is the basic method, but not everyone does it this way. Some boys prefer to just touch and stroke the sensitive tip of their penis. Others like to lie on their front and rub their whole body up and down against whatever they're lying on. When boys reach a peak of excitement, they have an orgasm and ejaculate – semen comes out of their penis. After a boy comes his penis will go limp and soft.
• Girls masturbate in many different ways too. Lots of girls find that their favourite way is to gently but firmly rub their clitoris at a steady, rhythmic pace, gradually getting faster. Others rub the whole vaginal area, or move one or two fingers around inside their vagina. Still others put a pillow between their legs and rub up and down against it, and some girls find that they can masturbate just by crossing their legs and squeezing them together in a regular rhythm, or by clenching and unclenching their vaginal muscles (the same ones you can use to stop your wee coming out mid-stream).

Like boys, most girls have orgasms once they reach their peak of sexual excitement. When they come, girls feel an explosive, pleasant feeling between their legs, and might notice that the muscles down there go into a little, twitchy spasm for a moment. Afterwards, there's a lovely feeling of release and relaxation, and the clitoris usually feels slightly tingly and sensitive.

I think the way I masturbate might be a bit strange . . .
Unlikely. So far we've only checked out the most basic ways of masturbating. There are a million and one more. Whatever it is you like to do, the chances are that it's harmless, normal, and is done by a squillion other people, too! Here are just a tiny handful of the things that people do.

• Touch, rub or squeeze their nipples.
• Stroke, touch or squeeze their balls.
• Use soapy water, oil, cream or some other slippery liquid on their hands or genitals to make their movements smoother.
• Put an object into their vagina.
• Put their fingers or an object into their bums (girls *and* boys).
• Rub their penises in and out of toilet roll tubes, soft fruit and many other inventive items!
• Spray their clitorises with a strong jet of water, using a shower attachment or tap.
• Rub themselves against furniture, cushions, soft toys and other things.
• Sit on or press themselves up against something that vibrates (like a washing machine, dryer or other piece of machinery).

And all those things are OK?
Yeah, they're normal, and they're generally safe as long as you follow these simple rules:

• Don't let any coloured or perfumed liquid go on your privates in case it irritates them or causes a rash – choose something gentle and pure, like spit, baby oil, butter, cooking oil, a gentle soap, Vaseline or KY Jelly (from chemists).
• If you're going to put your fingers into your vagina or bottom, make sure they're clean.
• If you're going to put something other than fingers inside yourself, make sure it's clean, has no sharp edges and won't

break. Never use anything made of glass or china. Go for something organic, like a vegetable (carrots are popular!), or something smooth and plastic).

• If you lose your grip on something you've put inside your vagina, don't panic. You can't lose anything up there, because it's only a few centimetres long and has a wall of flesh at the top. Relax, then gently slide your forefinger and thumb into your vagina (a little spit or other lubrication makes the job easier), 'bear down' like you were trying to poo, and grasp the object. If you don't manage, keep trying – you'll get it eventually. Failing that, a doctor won't mind fishing it out for you, and won't be embarrassed about it (although you probably will be!). If it's any comfort, doctors and hospitals get regular visits from people claiming that they just happened to be sitting naked on a chair when they mysteriously fell off onto this candle/carrot/courgette!

• If you're going to put something in your bottom, the same safety rules apply, plus you should be *ultra-careful* never to use something small enough to get lost or stuck up there. Unlike a vagina, your bottom is an open passage that just keeps on going (it's basically a continuation of your lower intestine). If you lose your grip on something, it could get horribly lost. This would be quite dangerous, and you'd definitely need to visit the doctor or the A and E department at a hospital.

• If you use a shower or tap, be very careful not to let it squirt water directly *into* your vagina, as a strong jet being forced up inside you is bad news.

• If you enjoy sticking your penis into things, please choose your object with safety in mind. Cardboard tubes and fruit are safe, as is any other unbreakable item that is smooth and has a hole at both ends. Things made of glass or china aren't safe. Neither are jars, wide-necked bottles and other things with a sealed bottom, because your thrusting could create a vacuum and you could end up getting your penis completely stuck.

- You may have heard jokes or even serious recommendations about sticking your penis into the end of the hoover nozzle and turning it on so that it 'sucks' you. Don't try it – it's dangerous.

- If you press up against electrical goods, please be sensible. Most large household appliances are perfectly OK, but industrial machinery is a total no-no – many a factory worker has met with a gruesome and tragic accident in the pursuit of fun!

Is it possible to suck your own penis?
Many boys give it a try for interest's sake, but unless you have a combination of a very supple spine, a very long penis and a conveniently shaped body, it's completely impossible and you're likely to end up with little more than a horribly strained back!

If putting something inside your vagina feels nice, does that mean that girls can get sexually excited when they use a tampon?
Many boys – and some girls – wonder about this. The answer is a resounding no, as anyone who has ever used a tampon can confirm. Sure, some objects feel nice going inside you, but a tampon is not one of them, because it's dry, soft and bendy. Useful, yes – exciting, no.

I masturbate a lot. Am I weird?
Not at all. Many teenagers masturbate a lot, and that's fine. If you're really worried, rest assured that it's unlikely that you'll wank this much for the rest of your life. Once you get into a relationship, have less time on your hands or just get a bit older, you're bound to do it less. Even if you carried on this way forever, though, it wouldn't be doing you any harm, so don't panic.

I'm not really into masturbating at all. Is there something wrong with me?

Nothing. Lots of people aren't into it, and that's just as normal as being very, very keen! Although we've gone into all the reasons why masturbation is normal and healthy, you're not really depriving yourself of anything if you don't do it.

Having said that, a lack of interest in masturbating can sometimes be a clue to some deeper problem, and if that's the case, it's important not to ignore it. For instance, if you feel that it's dirty or 'wrong' to feel sexual pleasure, your attitudes could make you feel sad and uncomfortable when you come to have a relationship, and it could be worth trying to talk to a counsellor at some point about how you feel. Similarly, if you feel funny about sexual touching because you've been sexually abused, getting the help of a professional will give you the chance to have a perfectly happy adult life – sexually and in every other way. For information about talking to a trained counsellor on the phone, or to arrange to see a counsellor in person, look at the *Counselling* section in Contacts and Resources at the back of the book.

Chapter 3

Attitudes to Sex

Coming to terms with all these new changes and discoveries can be pretty hard work. But don't pause for breath yet! Here's something else to get a handle on: attitudes. Everyone, including you, has their own ideas and opinions when it comes to sex, and it's important to think about these because they are going to strongly affect your life.

In this chapter, we look at:

- Your Parents' Attitudes
- Your Friends' Attitudes
- Changing Attitudes
- Sex and the Law
- Your Attitudes

Your Parents' Attitudes

Even the most broadminded parents find it tricky to cope with their kids growing up to be sexual adults. On the one hand they feel uncomfortable with the idea of you having sex (and it'll be impossible to understand how they feel until you have kids of your own). On the other hand, there are all the very real worries that this precious little person that they adore (that's you) is going to be running the risk of being made unhappy by a difficult sexual relationship, or getting pregnant, or catching a sexually transmitted infection.

Parents usually start worrying about all this stuff long before they even need to. It only takes the discovery of a wet-dream stain on the duvet or a poster of a scantily-clad pop star on the bedroom wall to convince most parents that their offspring are on the verge of shagging anything that moves.

Let's face it, most parents worry. They work themselves into a frenzy worrying and it's all because they care about you. Except they then go and show it in weird ways that wind you up, like being stroppy or saying embarrassing things. No matter how strict your parents are, the key to an easy home life is to talk to them. Hopefully, by talking to them, you can convince them that you are mature and knowledgeable enough to deal with all the problems and risks that come with sex. Most people are surprised how amenable their parents can turn out to be. Even if a parent doesn't like the idea of you having sex at all, most would rather know for sure who you were doing it with, where you were doing it and that you were using a condom, than be left in the dark to imagine the worst. If you talk to your parents from the start, you'll find that it'll be much easier to come to them for help and advice if you need it in the future.

Some parents have very strong views that young people

shouldn't have sex at all, or that sex should be saved for marriage. If you feel differently, this can be a problem. Changing their minds is likely to be impossible. In cases like this, you're best off keeping your thoughts and questions about sex secret, but that doesn't mean you should sneak around and go against what they say. Show your parents, if you can, that you are a mature and informed person, someone they can rely on to do the right thing. If you talk to them about everything else you get up to, come home when you say you're going to, and act as reasonably as you possibly can, they'll hopefully give you the trust and freedom you need for the moment, if not the permission to have sex yet. You'll just have to turn elsewhere for help and advice about sex. Try another, more approachable adult, like a different relative, a friend's parent, or a teacher. There are also some great helplines to call, for example Ask Brook (run by the Brook Advisory organisation) and the Muslim Community Helpline. They are confidential – ie they won't tell anyone that you called or what you talked about. Find their details in Contacts and Resources at the back of the book.

Your Friends' Attitudes

Coming of age sexually can put a big strain on friendships. Because everyone develops at different rates, there's always bound to be someone in every group who is so full of raging hormones that they're not interested in much else *but* sex, and someone else who'd still much rather be playing football, mucking around with their computer or looking at pictures of ponies. Everyone is wondering what everyone else thinks, and what can happen pretty fast is that everyone stops being honest about how they feel because they're so worried about being seen as 'normal'.

Beware of friends who set themselves up as sex experts. This is how some of the most dangerous and damaging myths and rumours about sex get spread around. Just because someone has done more than you sexually (or claims to have done), it doesn't mean that they know everything there is to know about sex. If someone tells you something, don't ever take it as gospel, especially if it sounds totally terrifying or too good to be true (like some amazingly simple way you can avoid getting pregnant). Check it out with an adult or in a book like the one you're reading!

The saddest thing that can happen is that someone can feel so pressured to keep up with what they *think* everyone else is doing, that they go and have sex just for the sake of it, only to discover later that all their friends are actually still virgins. Gaining sexual experience is not a competition, and losing your virginity doesn't make you a member of some elite club. It's all stuff that should be done at your own pace, when you're ready, and it shouldn't matter to a friendship if one person has 'gone further' than the other.

Peer Pressure

What we're talking about here is 'peer pressure'. Many girls and boys end up having sex before they really want to because of the pressure they feel from their own age group, and from older teenagers, to have sex. According to Brook Advisory, boys are twice as likely as girls to lose their virginity because of peer pressure from their mates. Girls are also likely to end up having sex before they want to because of pressure from their boyfriends, who are often older than them. Remember: NO ONE ever has a right to sex and EVERYONE has the right to say no to sex.

Other ways that your friends' attitudes can be a problem is if they are very different to yours. Everyone has their own point of view about subjects like virginity, sleeping around, being gay, abortion, pornography and a billion others. You and your mates are bound to clash on at least a few of them, but a true friendship can survive differences in opinion, as long as you're big enough to agree to disagree!

This is a time when platonic friendships can get a weeny bit strained, as you start wondering if your long-time pal fancies you – or indeed if you fancy them. Even if you decide there's nothing doing, it can be surprisingly tricky and envy-making when one of you starts dating. This doesn't mean your friendship is doomed, as long as you can talk honestly and act reasonably.

Changing Attitudes

It can be very weird when you notice that the snotty-faced kid from next door who you used to make mud-pies with has suddenly turned into a rampant sexual being who blatantly stares at your bum every time you walk past. Just as you're starting to get interested in people in a sexual way, they're starting to get interested in you too, and although being admired is a nice thing, it can be pretty weird, too.

Of course, it *does* all depend on how people show their feelings. If someone smiles at you in a friendly way or gives you a compliment, it can be a lovely, ego-boosting thing, even if you don't fancy them back. However, walking past a big group who are making rude gestures and noises or shouting out things like, 'Wouldn't mind giving you one!' and 'Show us your tits, babe!' can be one of the most completely horrible experiences in the world. In the past it's been mostly girls who have had to put up with this kind of thing, but these days you're just as likely to find a group of girls leering and making saucy comments at guys.

Young gays and lesbians may also find themselves targeted and may have to put up with comments and calls that range from the harmless-but-annoying to the downright insulting and frightening.

People who behave this way don't usually mean any harm – it's just a combination of wanting to have a laugh and 'bond' with their mates, and being too immature to know how to react when they find someone attractive, or when they encounter people who might be gay. But even though all that leering and yelling isn't supposed to be threatening or embarrassing, it can certainly feel like it to the person on the receiving end. At its worst, it can be a form of bullying.

The bottom line is that everyone has the right to walk down a street or a school corridor without being made to feel uncomfortable, so if you're guilty of this kind of thing, you need to stop it. If you're a victim of a leery gang, try to hold your head up high, smile and keep walking. Mostly this kind of attention is fairly harmless, but if it continues despite you asking them to stop, if it becomes more extreme and if it really distresses you, then it is *sexual harassment*. At this point adults need to be involved, and it has to be taken very seriously. See Chapter 13 for more details on sexual harassment and other unwanted sexual attention.

Sex and the Law

The powers that govern society also have an attitude to sex, and these are encoded in our laws. Here's a run-down of what they are.

Under 16s

In England, Scotland and Wales, the age at which you can legally engage in heterosexual sex (that is, sex between a male and a female) is sixteen. In Northern Ireland it's seventeen. These laws are there to protect you from having sex before you're mature enough to make your own decisions.

Gay and Lesbian Sex

In England, Scotland and Wales, sexual acts between men are legal over the age of sixteen, and over the age of seventeen in Northern Ireland. It's the same for sexual acts between women.

Prosecutions for Underage Sex

The Sexual Offences Act 2003 means that a person who has any kind of sexual contact with a person under the age of consent can be prosecuted. In reality, though, as long as the two people are of similar ages and there's no evidence that one partner has exploited the other, it's very unlikely that anyone under 16 will be prosecuted. The law is there to protect young people from harm and exploitation by adults. See Chapter 12 for more about sexual exploitation and sexual relationships with adults.

Your Attitudes to Sex

Even if you'd never really thought about it before, the chances are that you've already got pretty well-formed attitudes about sexuality. These attitudes have probably planted themselves in your head over the years without you even knowing it, and now that you're becoming a sexual person, it's the perfect time to drag them out, have a long hard look at them, and think them through properly. While everyone is entitled to their own opinion, there are ways of thinking that can make you go through life being thoughtless and unreasonable, hurting other people, and risking getting hurt yourself. Are you guilty of any of the deadly bad-attitude sins? Read on and find out.

Seeing Other People as Sex Objects

• Would you be prepared to have sex with someone who you thought was boring, dull or not very nice, just because they had a great body or attractive face?

• Would you consider it a waste of time to go out with someone who firmly refused to have sex, even if you really liked them?

• Do you think that a potential partner is 'only good for one thing'?

• Do you enjoy looking at pornography?

If you answered yes to two or more of these questions, it's quite likely that you do see people only as sex objects. While this isn't a terrible crime in itself, it's an attitude that can make you uncaring, and liable to treat others with less respect than they deserve. Even if you can't change the way you think, you can keep a check on how you behave. Using other people just for sex is a horrible thing. You not only risk hurting others, you also risk missing out on having truly fulfilling, happy relationships – because the best relationships (and the best sex) happen between two people who respect and trust each other equally. If you can't get that, get this: once people get wind of the fact that you're only after one thing and you don't mind treating your partners like dirt (and they will – people aren't stupid) you'll find that the chances of getting what you're after will rapidly diminish to nil.

Being Sexist

(This is not seeing boys and girls as 'equal', or assuming things about a person just because of their gender)

• Would you say that a girl was a 'whore', 'slut' or 'skank' because she sleeps around, but say he's 'sowing his wild oats' when talking about a boy?

• Do you think that most boys are just after sex and most girls are just after lovey-dovey stuff?

• If a boy turned down the chance to have sex, would you be surprised, or think he was weird?

If you answered yes to *any* of the above then you're guilty of thinking in a sexist way, at least some of the time. If you answered yes to all of them, it's pretty deeply ingrained. If you want to understand people and have a happy, unconfusing love-life, you've got to chuck out all your ideas about what girls and boys are *supposed* to be like and learn that everyone is different. There are lots of boys who'd rather have a kiss and a cuddle and wait until they get to really know and love someone before leaping into bed, and lots of girls who just adore having as much sex as possible. These people are not weirdos or sluts – they're perfectly normal. Wise up.

Believing There's Such a Thing as a 'Right' to Sex

• If someone gets into a steamy snogging session then refuses to go any further, are they a 'tease'?

• If you took someone on a fantastic date and spent a lot of money on them in the process, would it be fairly reasonable to expect sex, a feel, or at least a snog?

• If your partner had waited for months on end until you felt ready to have sex, but you still weren't 100% sure, should you do it anyway, as a 'thank you' for their patience and understanding?

Any 'yes' answers at all? You're guilty of believing that there are certain circumstances where people *should* have sex, even if they don't really want to. This is rubbish, and the kind of attitude which guarantees that someone is going to get hurt. Once again: *No one* ever has a right to sex and *everyone* has the right to say no to sex. That goes for kissing, groping and everything else, too. Intimate stuff should only happen when both people want it to. These facts are true no matter what the circumstances.

Being Homophobic
(Anti-gay)

• If your best friend told you they were gay, would you be put off being friends with them?

• Do you think that being gay is unnatural?

• Do you use words like 'bum-boy', 'poof', 'bender' or 'lezzie'?

• If you saw two men or two women kissing in public, would it bother you more than it would seeing a man and woman doing the same thing?

• Is there anything that straight people can do that you think gay people *shouldn't be* allowed to do (like joining a particular profession, adopting children, holding hands in public – anything)?

If you answered yes to two or more of the above, you're prejudiced against gay people, although you may not have even realised it. You probably picked up your ideas from your family, as you were growing up. Now's the time to start thinking for yourself. If you're bright, it's not hard to see the simple truth: everyone is equal, no matter what they get up to in their private lives.

Being Ignorant

• You're alone with someone you're crazy about and you're desperate to shag them, but neither of you has a condom. You might never get a chance like this again. Do you go ahead and do it?

• Do you think that you have little or no chance of getting a sexually transmitted infection (STI), even if you were to have sex without a condom?

• Is it true that if a boy gets very sexually excited, but can't do anything about it, he will be physically damaged in some way?

• Is it true that a girl is safe from the risks of pregnancy and disease during sex if the boy pulls his penis out quickly before he comes?

If you answered yes to any of the above, you're pretty ignorant about sex – in fact, you have some downright dangerous ideas. Being badly informed isn't your fault, but it's up to you now to be open-minded and prepared to learn the truth. Before you have a chance to put yourself or anyone else at risk, read this book very thoroughly!

Part 2
GEARING UP
FOR SEX

This part of the book is all about getting into gear for a sexual relationship. Are you fully sexually aware? Do the quiz to find out! Then get all the facts and equipment you need for safe sex – to protect you and your partner against pregnancy and STIs. Remember, when it comes to sex, preparation is everything!

Chapter 4

Are You Ready For Sex?

There's no exact age or time when you suddenly become ready to have sex. It's really about having done just the right amount of growing up, physically and mentally, and that can happen very early on for some people, and much later for others. The only person who can really tell if you're ready to have sex is you: it's your life, your body and, ultimately, your decision. This chapter is here to help you decide. In it you'll find:

- How Do You Know You're Ready?
- So . . . How Sexually Aware Are You? (Quiz)
- So What Am I Waiting For?
- Is Now the Right Time?
- Losing Your Virginity

How Do You Know You're Ready?

Let's answer some of those burning questions . . .

Surely you're as ready as you feel. If you want sex, why can't you just do it?

Wanting to have sex is not the same as being ready to have sex, although it's easy to get the two feelings confused. Once you've found out as much as you possibly can on the subject, examine yourself. Are you sure you're ready? Sex is a very big deal, and it's not just about the act itself. There's so much else to take into account – like your partner's needs and feelings as well as your own, understanding risks and problems, staying safe and being as aware and informed as possible. You need to be *certain* that you're ready for it, and not get into sexual situations before you are.

What's the big deal about being ready?

It's all about being clued up and prepared for sex. If you wait until you're ready, your early experiences should be happy, safe and fulfilling. If you don't, you risk feeling scared and confused and disappointed afterwards. And if you don't know or fully understand the ins-and-outs of sexual protection, you could also end up with an unwanted pregnancy or a nasty disease.

What makes someone ready to have sex?

You need to understand sex and relationships and what you want to get out of them. You need to be able to control your urges and think carefully before rushing into things. You need to know all about sex and safety. In other words, what we're really talking about here is *sexual awareness*. No one is born sexually aware and, unfortunately, it doesn't just come to you – you have to make it happen. You don't need to have sex to be sexually aware – in fact, the smartest people are sexually aware *long* before they hop into bed with anyone.

So . . . How Sexually Aware Are You?

The flow-chart on the following pages was specially devised by a sex-expert to help you find out how sexually aware you are at the moment. Start by answering the first question, following the 'yes' or 'no' path to the next question, and so on, until you get to one of the four conclusions.

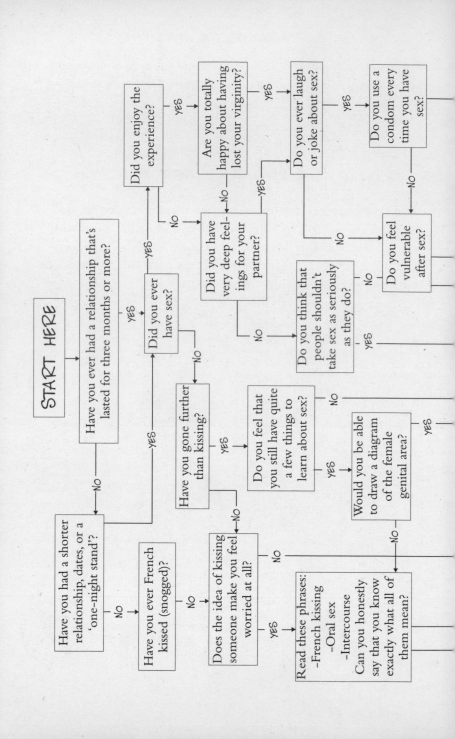

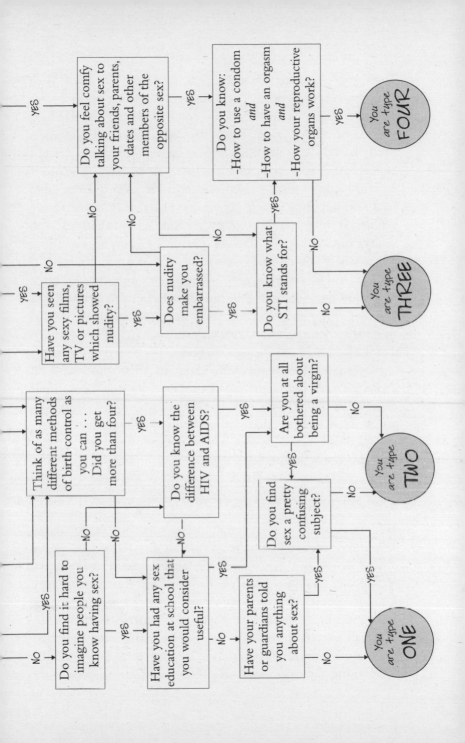

Type One – Inexperienced

You are: *Inexperienced* – and although some virgins are as sexually aware as those who *have* had sexual experiences, you're not one of them. Your knowledge of sexual matters is pretty basic, to say the least. Maybe you're not really interested in sex at the moment – which is fine – or perhaps you find it embarrassing to talk or think about. It seems as if no one has told you anything much about sex – or if they have, you've ignored it, forgotten it, or got the wrong end of the stick.

Try not to: Let your lack of knowledge and understanding of sex worry you or embarrass you – it'll come with a tiny bit of time and effort. However, it's dead important at this stage that you don't decide to find out more by actually getting into a sexual situation with someone – you need to find out and understand quite a bit of stuff on your own first if you want to avoid a potentially difficult experience.

Try to: Ignore friends who claim to know more and do more, sexually, than you do – the chances are that half of their claims are made up, and there's no point in comparing yourself to other people anyway. If you want to talk about sex, choose someone older and wiser instead. Whatever you do, read this book thoroughly!

Type Two – A Smart, Clued-Up Virgin

You are: A member of a very admirable breed – a *smart, clued-up virgin*. Although you're very sexually aware, you have chosen not to put your knowledge into practice yet, and you feel pretty happy with your decision. You're obviously interested in sex, as you have clearly gone out of your way to find out and digest lots of important information about it, from all sorts of sources. You might sometimes feel that there are a few things you're not 100% clear on – especially concerning the emotional side of sex and relationships – but you're probably aware that what you know already is plenty for now, and the rest will come in good time.

Try not to: Feel under any pressure to lose your virginity. Your attitude, intelligence and savvy prove that you're a mature person, so you should never feel tempted to rush into sex just to 'keep up' with your friends.

Try to: Carry on living in the sensible, grown-up and well-paced way you've been doing already. Wait for someone who you feel is just the right person to share your first sexual experience with – someone as bright and wise as you – and you'll be all set for a happy, healthy future sex life.

Type Three – Sexually Experienced but not Sexually Aware

You are: *Sexually experienced but not sexually aware* – a rather dodgy state to be in. Losing your virginity counts for very little when you don't really understand what you've done or what you're doing. You never gave yourself a chance to understand sex – or what you wanted out of it – before trying it, and the chances are that your experiences haven't been happy or safe.

Try not to: Get any further into deep waters before you've educated yourself some more. Learn as much as you can, as soon as possible. Luckily you've got this book to help you. Read it carefully and take it all in.

Try to: Get your head together before you have sex again. Feeling more knowledgeable should help, but if you've lost your sense of self respect, you've got to regain it before you risk getting into another sexual situation. If your past experiences have disturbed you, it would be a good idea to talk about this to an adult that you trust – if not your parents, then a friend's parent or a teacher. Or you could call Ask Brook on 0808 802 1234 or Childline on 0800 111.

Equally importantly, you've got to choose more carefully who you have sex with in the future, for your own sake. Whoever it's been so far has either been as much in the dark as you are, or else has been a careless sort who hasn't bothered to get to know you or think about your welfare – either way, not a good choice of partner.

Type Four – Very Sexually Aware

You are: *Very sexually aware* – not just because of your experience, but because you are well-informed, and able to understand everything you've learnt along the way. You know a lot about sex, so you aren't afraid of it, and you also have a good, relaxed attitude which means that you feel able to discuss sex honestly and freely with others. This ability to chat openly helps you to learn even more about sex.

Try not to: Show off about your sexual knowledge or assume that because you have the sex thing sussed, you also know everything there is to know about relationships. Being sexually aware doesn't mean that you necessarily fully understand the emotional side of things yet, which can be just as tricky and mystifying as the sexual side.

Try to: Carry on as you are, because you're doing great, but always be cautious, and open to learning and growing – don't close yourself off by assuming that you know it all already.

So What Am I Waiting For?

Once you're sure that you're ready to cope with sex, and all the complications it can bring into your life, the big questions are when, where and with who? Some people hit this point desperate to 'get rid of' their virginity, and don't really care what the circumstances are. This doesn't spell certain disaster, but it's not a great attitude to kick off your sex life with. After all, sex isn't just about *you* – it's a shared experience between two people. If you can wait until exactly the right person comes along, you've got a much better chance of having a happy, fun and safe first time.

These days not everyone waits until they're married or engaged to have sex, but most agree that this idea is based on quite a sound wisdom: that if you love and trust someone enough to want to spend a big chunk of your life with them, then they're bound to be a pretty good choice of person to trust your all-important first experience to. Even if you don't plan to wait until you've found a life-long partner (you might not ever want a life-long partner!), it's still a good idea to pick someone you get along with, know well, trust, and want to have a longish relationship with. If you lose your virginity after just a couple of dates – or indeed with someone you just met at a party – there's a good chance that the relationship won't last much past the first bonk. No matter how tough you are, this can be difficult to cope with once you've shared such an intimate experience as sex.

You should never worry about 'missing' an opportunity to lose your virginity. It's far better to wait until you're absolutely certain you want to go ahead, than to rush into things and regret it later. If the person you were thinking about having sex with isn't prepared to wait, or give you another chance in the future, then they probably weren't a great bet anyway.

The very worst way to lose your virginity is when you're so drunk or out of it that you don't know what's going on. If you deliberately get wasted because you're nervous about sex, then you're definitely not ready, and should wait until the prospect seems less terrifying. The statistics say it all – four out of ten thirteen and fourteen year olds lost their virginity when drunk or high on drugs; and one in five had sex they regretted after drinking. Having sex when you're drunk or high on drugs is often a frightening and unpleasant experience, as well as being dangerous – you're less likely to use contraceptive protection, so putting yourself and your partner at risk of pregnancy or STIs, and more likely to get hurt and worse (see *Alcohol and Drugs* in Chapter 12 for more information). You need to aim to be completely sober when you lose your virginity – and it will certainly be a more enjoyable experience that way.

Is Now the Right Time?

If you're considering taking a relationship further – ie, having sex – not just for the first time, but any time, you should always ask yourself these questions:

• Are we both sixteen or over?

• Do I *really* like, fancy, care about or maybe even love my prospective partner?

• Do they like, fancy, care about or maybe even love me, too?

• If I don't feel like I want to have sex now, would my partner be prepared to wait until I do?

• Am I certain that my partner is OK about us using a condom?

• Have I or my partner got a condom already, or is one of us prepared to go out and buy some before we decide to have sex?

Now ask yourself these:
- Is there any possibility that my partner is 'just after one thing' and might dump me afterwards?
- Has my partner ever put me under any pressure to go further than I really wanted to?
- Has my partner ever threatened or implied that they might leave me if I don't have sex?
- If my partner *had* threatened to leave me if I wouldn't have sex, would I go ahead and have sex anyway, even if I didn't want to?
- Is wanting to 'keep up' with my friends an important factor in my decision?
- Is wanting to 'get rid of' my virginity an important factor?

If you answered a definite 'yes' to all of the first set of questions and a definite 'no' to all the questions in the second set, then you're onto a winner. You've got all the ingredients for a happy, safe sexual experience, and should feel free to start as soon as you feel like it!

If you answered 'no' to any of the questions in the first section, or 'yes' to any in the second, put the brakes on. The chances are that things will turn out fine, but you need to think the situation through and get to know your partner better first.

If you have sex for dodgy reasons, with a dodgy person or without taking precautions against pregnancy and disease, you're not doing yourself any favours, to say the least. Not only could you end up miserable, confused or worse, but you're also sending an invisible message to your partner – and the rest of the world that says: 'Hello! I don't think I'm worth much! Look at me – I don't care what happens to me! Feel free to use me, why don't you!'

Choosing the right time to have sex is really all about having self-respect – the most important thing anyone can have.

What if I don't get a chance to think carefully before I have sex?
That happens. You might be in a very intimate situation – alone with someone, having a heavy, passionate snogging and petting session and suddenly you realise that you're on the verge of losing your virginity. In these cases, you just have to go with your gut instinct – do you *really* want to do it? Not because all your friends have, not because you're scared of losing your partner, not because you figure you 'might as well' now you're this close to it, nor because you're worried about being a 'tease' if you back out, but because you *really, really* want to experience sex and closeness with this person, *right* now? If the answer is a definite yes, then as long as one of you has a condom ready to use, there's no reason why you shouldn't go ahead.

Losing Your Virginity

No matter how aware or well-prepared you are, everyone worries just a bit about their first time. Here are some of the most common frets . . .

Can someone tell if you're a virgin?
Not by looking at you, no.

What about during sex?
Not necessarily. Boys have no physical signs of virginity at all. The only physical sign of virginity for girls is the hymen – a thin piece of skin that grows across the entrance to the vagina. Not all girls are born with a hymen, and for those that are, not all still have them when they come to have sex for the first time. If they do, it can feel like a sort of barrier. It breaks quite easily and sometimes bleeds a little bit. If the girl's partner notices this (which he might not)

then he *would* know she was a virgin. However, most girls' hymens break before they lose their virginity, usually without them even knowing it. This can be caused by a thousand things, including putting something in the vagina (like a tampon) or doing something physical that involves stretching your legs apart – like horse riding, bike-riding, climbing a tree or doing gymnastics.

Couldn't someone tell that you were inexperienced?
Yes, perhaps. If your partner had had sex in the past with someone who was experienced, they might be able to make a comparison and tell the difference. Inexperienced boys often come more quickly, although many experienced boys – and men – come quickly too, so it's not a foolproof sign. Inexperienced girls usually move around less and seem more inhibited and shy than experienced ones – though, again, the same goes for some experienced females. But even if someone could tell that you were inexperienced, they wouldn't know if you were a virgin or not.

If you don't want your partner to know that you're a virgin, you should ask yourself why not. If you're in a loving relationship, then your partner should be flattered, even overjoyed, that you've chosen them to be the very, very special person who shares your first sexual experience. If you really don't like the idea of them knowing, then perhaps they're not a great choice of partner. After all, if you don't feel comfortable enough to tell them something that important, how the heck are you going to feel relaxed enough to enjoy sex with them?

I don't like using tampons, and when I've tried putting my fingers inside myself, more than one hurts and feels too big. I'm worried that my vagina will be too small to fit a penis inside it . . .
Don't worry. It's virtually unheard of for a girl's vagina to be

too small for sex. We're talking about a remarkably stretchy organ, that can comfortably expand to fit any penis, no matter how long or wide it is. Just remember, a vagina can stretch enough to let a baby out – and no guy on the planet has a penis the size of a baby, anyway! Some boys like to brag by warning girls that their penis might be 'too big' for them. This is a load of old guff – ignore it.

Does losing your virginity hurt?
It varies. Most boys and many girls find it doesn't hurt at all. Most girls and a few boys find that it hurts just a little bit when the penis first goes in, but then it's absolutely fine. Some girls find the whole thing quite painful. Both boys and girls can feel a little bit sore afterwards.

Generally, though, losing your virginity never hurts enough to put you off sex!

Is there anything you can do to make it hurt less?
Yes, several things. Firstly, it's worth knowing that the more damp the vagina is, the easier and less painful it is for the penis to slip in. If a girl is happy, relaxed and sexually excited she makes her own natural *lubrication* (wetness). This is what people mean when they talk about a girl *getting wet*. Your condom should come ready-lubricated (with spermicide or lubricant) and this helps too. You can also buy lubricants from the chemist – just be sure to choose one like KY jelly that doesn't weaken your condom. See more about condoms in the Chapter 5.

Sex can be more painful if the girl is tensing up all the muscles in her vagina – another reason why it's important for the girl to feel relaxed. If you can't relax, it's still possible to relax your vaginal muscles if you concentrate.

Will my partner enjoy having sex with me if I'm a virgin and I don't know what to do?

If you're both virgins, then at least you won't have to worry about being compared to any of your partner's previous conquests. If your partner isn't a virgin, though, it still shouldn't make any difference to them. For a start, a lot of girls and boys find the idea of being the first person to make love to someone else very ego-boosting and sexy. Secondly, if they care about you, then they're having sex to get closer to you, so they'll enjoy it whatever happens. Bear in mind too, that they fancy you and will be very turned on by seeing and feeling your body and getting close to you, so it's going to be neither here nor there if you're not swinging from the light fitments or practising ancient eastern sex rituals.

Will I enjoy losing my virginity?

Hopefully! It's unlikely that the earth will move, fireworks will go off and you'll suddenly think, 'Aha! So this is what all the fuss is about!', because those feelings usually come when you're *really* comfortable with your partner, your own body and having sex. That said, experiencing the magical closeness of sex with someone you really like can be – and should be – wonderful from the word go, and if you're lucky, it'll be very sexually exciting too. If you're a girl (or even if you're a boy), you can't definitely expect to have an orgasm – but hopefully it'll be a really pleasurable experience anyway. The after-effects of losing your virginity can be very nice too – you often feel closer to your partner and more worldly. Most adults agree, looking back, that their first sexual experience is never their best, but most enjoy it a lot, anyway . . . And isn't it nice to know that it just keeps getting better and better?

Chapter 5

Contraception

Let's get two facts straight right away:
  • Getting a sexually transmitted infection (STI) is no fun at all, and can be very serious.
  • An unwanted pregnancy can ruin your life.
If you have sex, you risk getting an STI, getting pregnant or getting someone else pregnant, unless you take proper precautions.

In this chapter we're looking at:

  • Pregnancy
  • Myths About Contraception
  • Getting Clued Up About Contraception
  • Whose Responsibility – His or Hers?
  • Where to Go For Contraception
  • Types of Contraception

If you think you know it all already, you could be wrong. Read it anyway.

Pregnancy

Pregnancy happens when a sperm meets up with a ripe female egg. You don't have to be a genius to work out that it's pretty easy to get pregnant, especially if you know the facts:

• Every time a boy comes, he sets free literally *millions* of sperm.

• A girl releases just one egg a month, but it's ripe to be fertilised (joined by a sperm) for between one and three days.

• It's nearly impossible for a girl to tell exactly when her eggs are released.

• Sperm can live inside a girl for ages – five days is quite normal – so even if there's no ripe egg on the day that a girl has sex, there could still be plenty of sperm about when it finally turns up.

• Teenage girls are very fertile, and Britain has the highest teenage pregnancy rate in Europe.

Find out more about getting pregnant in Chapter 11.

Myths About Contraception

There are plenty of myths about how you can avoid pregnancy without using *contraception,* or birth control. Some are based on misunderstandings of the truth, others are just nonsense invented by idiots. Perhaps you've heard you can't get pregnant if:

. . . it's your first time.

. . . your partner masturbates before having sex.

. . . you have sex standing up.

. . . you don't have an orgasm.

. . . you jump up and down a lot afterwards.

. . . you wee afterwards.

. . . you have a bath afterwards.

. . . you wash your vagina out with a fizzy cola drink afterwards. (This one is stupid twice over – it won't stop you getting pregnant and it's also a bad idea from a health point of view. Flooding your vagina can be dangerous.)

These are all pretty silly, but they've stuck around for years and years because people go on believing them, and telling their friends all about them. If people can believe those, then it's no surprise that they also buy the myths which sound quite logical and sensible. How about:

. . . the safe time – the belief that a girl can't get pregnant during her period? Although a girl is less likely to get pregnant during her period, it's by no means impossible. Don't risk it.

. . . the myth that a girl can't get pregnant if she hasn't yet started her periods? Untrue – a girl will ovulate (release a ripe egg) before her first period.

. . . the withdrawal method, also known as *being careful* – the belief that if a boy pulls his penis out before he comes, his partner can't get pregnant because the semen doesn't go inside her? What's so scary about this is that *so many* people – adults included – think that it's true, when it's actually complete nonsense. In fact, a little bit of semen – known as *pre-ejaculate* – almost always sneaks out long before the big spurt happens. It's usually an amount so small that you wouldn't notice it, but the scary truth is that this tiny bit of spunk contains loads of sperm. A girl can get pregnant this way even if the penis only enters the vagina for a very short amount of time.

Natural Family Planning

Natural Family Planning, or the Natural Method of contraception, is not a myth, but it *is* so often misunderstood that it can result in many unwanted pregnancies and misery. Let's be clear about what the Natural Method is, and what it isn't.

- Some people think that the Natural Method is the Withdrawal Method – see opposite. It isn't.

- Some people think that the Natural Method means you can have sex safely during a girl's period – see above again. It isn't.

- You cannot use the Natural Method unless you have been taught how to by a specialist Natural Family Planning teacher.

- It works by finding out when the woman's most fertile phase is (the time of month she's most likely to make a baby) and avoiding unprotected sex during this time. The system involves observing and recording her body's different natural signs, every day of her cycle for six months.

- Every woman is different and so no two women's fertile phases are going to be the same. This is why a special teacher needs to teach women how to use the method – you can't do it on your own.

- The natural method will not protect you from STIs.

- It's a lot of work and quite complicated.

- It works best for couples who are in long-term relationships, don't mind the risk of getting pregnant and who have both been checked and found clear of STIs.

- Doctors wouldn't generally recommend this method for teenagers.

All this brings us back to square one. There's simply no alternative to using proper birth control. So what kind of contraception should you use? There's certainly lots of choice, but before we check it out, there's another very important thing to consider. You don't just need to protect against pregnancy . . .

If you're having sex, you're also at risk of getting a sexually transmitted infection (STI). We talk about these in detail in Chapter 6.

Getting Clued Up About Contraception

The only way to be 100% sure that you won't get pregnant or contract an STI is not to have any sexual contact. So if you are going to have sex, it is vital that know all about contraception before you do anything. You need to plan ahead and use the right contraceptives to protect you and your partner.

Unfortunately, no method of contraception is 100% fail-safe. Pregnancies can sometimes happen even when contraception is used. That's why it's essential that you are as clued up and aware as possible before you start having sex.

Whose Responsibility – His or Hers?

There are a lot of different methods of birth control available, but apart from condoms, all of them are designed to be used by girls. Despite this, contraception is the responsibility of *both* partners. A boy should never assume that birth control is nothing to do with him. He owes it to his girlfriend to give her any help and support she needs in choosing the right method for them. Beware of boys (and girls) who are not prepared to be responsible about contraception – who are happy to have sex without using a condom or any other method of birth control. Never have sex in these circumstances. Always be prepared – *both* of you!

Where To Go for Contraception

On the NHS all contraception is free and contraceptive advice is confidential, which means that the doctor or nurse you see will not tell anyone that you visited or what you saw them for. You can go to:

- Your GP.
- Another GP if you'd prefer, and register for contraception only.
- A Brook Centre – these centres provide advice for under-twenty-fives on all aspects of sexual health and contraception.
- A family planning clinic.
- A young person's clinic.

Ring the fpa (Family Planning Association) on 0845 122 8690 to find your nearest young person's clinic, or visit their website at www.fpa.org.uk. To find your nearest Brook centre visit their website – www.brook.org.uk – or phone Ask Brook on 0808 802 1234.

Types of Contraception

Please be aware that the information given here is a general guide to contraception, and must not be relied upon as a substitute for medical advice. Contraception is a personal thing and different methods suit different people for both medical and personal reasons. Because of this, you must never obtain, lend or borrow contraception for other people. This could be very dangerous – you are risking your own health and theirs, as well as the possibility of an unwanted pregnancy.

Many of the methods of contraception listed below are 'hormonal methods' (both kinds of contraceptive pill, the injection, patch and implant, the IUS and the emergency pill). All these methods rely on taking hormones to prevent pregnancy. Because they alter your hormone levels, they can cause side-effects and come with some risk to your health. They are not going to suit everyone.

It may take a little experimenting before you find the right contraception for you and your partner. So being as well-informed as possible is absolutely essential! For any information about contraception not covered in this chapter, phone Ask Brook on 0808 802 1234 or the fpa on 0845 122 8690. Your call will be confidential – this means they won't tell anyone about it.

Before we get started, remember these very important facts:

The only contraceptive that protects against pregnancy *and* STIs is a CONDOM. The only way to stay safe is to use a condom *every time* you have sex.

Male and Female Condoms

Condoms are a brilliant invention. They're small and easy to carry around and they're the key to being able to have sex without playing Russian roulette with your life. A male condom is a penis-shaped tube made of very thin latex rubber. It keeps the boy's semen in and everything else out, so both the wearer and his partner are protected both against pregnancy and STIs. There is also a female condom

(Femidom), which a girl inserts into her vagina. It works in the same way as a male condom – by preventing sperm from entering the vagina.

How do you use a male condom?
Male condoms come in little square individual wrappers. All condoms come with instructions, so read these carefully first. When you take the condom out of its wrapper it's rolled up very tightly, so that it looks like a little circle with a raised ring round the edge, and a small bobble in the middle. Don't unroll it! Here's how to put one on properly:

• Hold the condom by the tip (the bobble in the middle), squeezing out any air that might be in it, and place it on the end of the penis.

• Gently place your thumb and forefinger on either side of the raised ring round the edge, and start rolling the whole thing down. You can use your other hand to help, if you need to. If it won't roll easily, it's on upside down – start again.

• Always unroll a condom carefully, being careful not to tear it, especially if you've got long nails. Once the condom is completely unrolled, and feels perfectly snug, you're ready to rock!

• When you've used a condom: straightaway after the boy has come, and while his penis is still quite hard (otherwise the condom could become loose enough to leak semen out, or actually come off inside his partner), he needs to hold the condom onto the base of his penis while pulling out of his partner. Then he can remove the condom and tie a knot at the open end of it to contain the semen. Wrap up the used condom and bin it – don't flush it down the loo (our sewage system can't cope with them).

• Remember – don't ever use a condom that has passed its sell-by date.

How effective is the male condom at preventing pregnancy?
A male condom is 98% effective if used according to instructions. This means 2 out of 100 women who use them properly will get pregnant each year. Used less carefully, there is more risk of pregnancy.

What makes the male condom less effective at preventing pregnancy?
 • Male condoms can split or tear, letting sperm through. As soon as he's come, the boy needs to withdraw his penis as described above. If not, sperm can leak out, or the condom can come off inside the girl.
 • The boy's penis can touch the girl's vagina before they put a condom on, and sperm might enter her this way.
 • A condom can slip off, letting sperm into the vagina.
 • It may not have been put on correctly.
 • It can be damaged by sharp fingernails or jewellery. Using *spermicide* as well as a condom can help reduce the risk of pregnancy in these cases. Spermicide is a chemical jelly or foam that kills sperm, and is used together with other forms of contraception for extra safety. Spermicide also makes a good lubricant – that is, it helps the penis slip in more easily and can make sex more comfortable. While we're on the subject of lubricants, it's important to know that most household or beauty products (such as oils or creams) are a total no-no: they can weaken or dissolve the latex that condoms are made of. If you want a lubricant that's not a spermicide, get one that's been designed for the job, such as KY jelly.

What are the advantages of the male condom?
 • They protect both partners against some STIs as well as pregnancy.
 • There are no side-effects (unless you're allergic to latex rubber or spermicide).

- You only need use them when you want to have sex.
- Male condoms are easy to get hold of.
- Male condoms come in all shapes and sizes, so every boy can find one to suit them.

What are the disadvantages of the male condom?

- Occasionally people are allergic to the latex rubber that regular condoms are made from, or to the spermicide that coats them. Ask your pharmacist or at a family planning clinic for a polyurethane alternative, if this is the case. Polyurethane condoms come without spermicide.
- Putting on a male condom interrupts sex.
- Some boys lose their erection when they put a condom on.
- They can be tricky to put on, and to keep on – make sure you practise beforehand! See tips on page 87 for how to do this.

Where can I get the male condom?

Condoms and spermicide are free from family planning, sexual health clinics and young people's clinics such as Brook. You can also buy condoms, spermicide and lubricants cheaply from pharmacies, petrol stations and supermarkets, and there are often condom dispensing machines in the toilets and hallways of pubs, restaurants, youth clubs, cinemas and leisure centres.

What is a female condom?

A female condom is like a slim bag made of polyurethane. It has a rubber ring at the closed end, and another, wider ring at the open end. Instead of going over a penis, it goes inside a girl's vagina and is held in place by the larger ring that lies outside the vagina. It gives the same protection against disease and pregnancy as a condom, and it works in roughly the same way.

How do you use the female condom?

• Read the instructions on the packet carefully first. They will tell you how the condom works and how to put it on, with diagrams.

• Put in the condom before the penis has any contact with your genitals. You can do this any time before sex, which can be quite handy!

• To insert the condom, lie down, squat, or put one leg up on a chair, whichever is more comfortable.

• Squeeze the inner ring between your thumb and middle finger. Keep your index finger in the centre of this ring to hold it steady.

• Spread your vaginal lips with your other hand, then push the squeezed ring as far up your vagina as you can.

• Put a finger inside the condom and push the inner ring as far back as it will go.

• The outer ring should be outside your vagina, next to the skin.

• You and your partner may need to guide his penis in to make sure it doesn't slip down the side.

• When you've finished, twist the outer ring closed to keep in the semen then pull the condom out. Wrap it and bin it – don't flush it down the loo.

Be careful that the condom doesn't slip about when you're having sex. And as with male condoms, don't use it past its sell-by date and never reuse it.

How effective are female condoms in preventing pregnancy?

A female condom is 95% effective if used according to instructions. This means that five in a hundred women who use the female condom properly will get pregnant each year.

What makes the female condom less effective at preventing pregnancy?
- The boy's penis can slip around the side of it on entry.
- It can fall out.
- It may not have been put in correctly.
- It can be damaged by sharp finger nails or jewellery.

What are the advantages of the female condom?
- It protects both partners against STIs.
- There are no side effects – and as it's made of polyurethane, a female condom can be used by people who are allergic to latex rubber.
- Because it's made of polyurethane, you can use an oil-based lubricant and not damage it.
- You only need to use one when you want to have sex.
- It can go in any time before sex.
- It's good for boys who lose their erection in a male condom.

What are the disadvantages of the female condom?
- It can be tricky to put in properly, and to keep in place during sex if you're not used to it.
- Not all clinics stock the female condom and they're more expensive to buy than male ones.

Where can I get the female condom?
Female condoms are free from some (but not all) family planning clinics. You can also buy them from pharmacies.

More questions about condoms

What if I'm too embarrassed to buy condoms?
If you're not embarrassed to have sex, then there's no reason why you should be embarrassed to buy condoms. Just go into

a shop, look for them, pick up a packet and pay. It's no more embarrassing than buying batteries, tissues or anything else, and no one is going to ask you any questions. Or why not get them from a dispensing machine? You can always wait until there's no one else around.

Better still, go to your GP, local family planning clinic, young person's clinic or Brook centre, and get some for free!

Which condom should I use?
The most important thing to look for when you're choosing a male condom is safety and quality. Only use condoms with the BSI 'kite mark' or CE mark on it, which means they've been through tough testing and are top quality. You can also be sure that you're onto a safe bet if you choose condoms made by a well-known companies like Durex, Mates or Jiffi.

You'll see lots of different types of male condom, with all sorts of strange names and descriptions, including brightly-coloured ones (a bit of fun) and flavoured ones (not a bad idea if you're using them for oral sex or want to try putting them on with your mouth, as most regular condoms taste gross). There's no 'best' type of condom – it's a matter of personal taste, and most people try a few different ones before settling with one they like. As a rough guide, though, many guys prefer ultra-thin ones (sometimes called 'gossamer') because they say they can feel more, and it's also very smart to go for a condom that is coated with a spermicide. If you pick condoms without spermicide, you might want to buy some spermicide to use with them, for extra protection.

So far there's only one make of female condom – the Femidom. You *can* use oil-based lubricants with the female condom, as it's made of polyurethane, not latex.

When should I buy male or female condoms?
Well before you get an opportunity to use them! You don't

have to be certain that you're going to have sex to buy condoms. It's better to buy them just in case and hang on to them for a bit than to be caught short. If you feel ready to have sex, and you're going out on dates where you hope very much that you'll be lucky, it's time to get yourself some condoms. If you're in a steady relationship and you seem to be going a little bit further every time you get together, it's *definitely* time. Keep at least one wrapped condom in the bag or jacket you use regularly, and at least one in your room. Make sure you don't bend the packet – this can damage the condom inside. Condoms have a fairly long shelf-life, so don't worry too much if they sit gathering dust for a while – you're bound to use them eventually, and you'll be ever so glad you had them. All the same, always remember to check the use-by date on the packet and throw out any that have passed it!

When should you put a condom on?
Male condoms: after the boy's penis has become erect, but long before it goes anywhere near his partner's genitals.

Female condoms: any time you like before the boy's penis has come in contact with your genitals. Even before you've gone out on a date together! The good thing about the female condom is that you can put it in on your own before you intend to have sex, so you needn't feel 'on show' by having to put it in at a crucial moment!

Should the boy put a condom on himself?
Not necessarily. His partner could do it, or they could do it together. Actually, lots of couples find that putting on a condom is a sexy, nice experience, and see it as a part of love-making. The same could go for putting in a female condom! It's all part of getting to know each other.

Is it difficult to put on/in a condom?

Not really – the more you do it, the easier it gets, and that goes for male *and* female condoms. It's a good idea to get some condoms to practise with *before* you have sex, because the more confident you are with them, the less chance there is of having an embarrassing, fumbling experience when it comes to the real thing. If you're a boy, you've already got all the equipment you need to practise. If you're a girl, practise putting a male condom on a carrot, banana or candle, or just a couple of your fingers. If you're a girl who wants to use a female condom, have a go at the different ways of putting one in (squatting, leg up on a chair, etc) to find the best position for you. Practise makes perfect – whatever type of condom you're using, you need to know that you can use it properly, safely and with confidence!

If you've used a male or female condom for practising, chuck it out afterwards: it's no good for sex once it's been unrolled and fiddled with.

Someone told me that you can put a male condom on with your mouth. Is that true?

Yes, a boy's partner can do this as a bit of sexy fun! It takes practise, but the general idea is to unwrap the condom, place it just behind your teeth with the tip facing inwards, then open wide and plonk it onto your partner's penis. Once it's sitting there safely, you can start unrolling by pressing your lips together just above the raised ring and slowly lowering your mouth down the shaft. Don't choke yourself – you can finish the job with your tongue!

Do people think that a girl who carries a condom is 'easy'?

Anyone with half a brain would think that a girl who carried a condom was very mature and smart. Anyone who thinks otherwise is a tosser, and not worth worrying about.

I'd like to keep some condoms just in case, but I'm scared of my parents finding them . . .

Some parents would indeed throw a wobbly if they discovered your condoms, because they'd assume that you were having sex, and be put out that they didn't know anything about it.

Hopefully, though, once they got over the shock, they'd feel relieved that you were taking all the proper precautions and go easy on you.

If your parents are easy-going, you could try talking to them about your plans – then you won't have to worry about being found out. If you really can't talk to them, then you'll just have to hide the condoms very well. Whatever, don't let the fear of being found out put you off. Your safety is the most important thing, and it's better to have condoms and risk a parental strop than not to have them at all.

When should I mention condoms to my partner?

If you're in a proper relationship and you've talked about having sex, or are actually planning it, then it's obviously a close, mature relationship and you can mention condoms when you're chatting.

If you're not that relaxed with your partner yet, but it looks like you're going to have sex anyway, you should take the initiative. First, make sure you've got a condom handy in case your partner hasn't. Wait until you're pretty sure that sex is on the cards, but not so late that there's no turning back. If you're on your own, with no chance of being disturbed, you've been snogging and petting for a while, one or both of you have shed a few items of clothing, and whoever's got the penis has an erection – then it's definitely time to stop and mention condoms.

But what do I say?

You could start with a simple, friendly, 'Wait a minute . . .', then say, 'Do you think I should get a condom for us?' Alternatively, stop and get the condom out, then say, 'I think I should put this on . . .' or 'I think you should put this on . . .' It all sounds rather scary, because it's a bit like saying, 'OK, it's shagging time!' and there's always the chance that your partner wasn't planning to go that far. It doesn't really matter, though — at least you've made it clear that when you eventually have sex, you won't do it without a condom. If your partner is bright, they'll be relieved — it was probably on their mind too.

What if my partner doesn't like condoms?
If someone refuses to wear a condom, or says they don't want you to wear one, it's time to stop and think long and hard about that person and your relationship with them. Refusing to use a condom is like saying, 'I don't care about you and your safety, and I don't care about myself, either.' Do you really want to share your affections and your body with someone who is that stupid and thoughtless? Even if you fancy them like crazy, or you're terrified that you'll lose them if you make a fuss, it's not worth it. You've got to stand up for yourself and your safety. If you show your partner that you respect yourself enough to put your foot down over this, they should respect you back.

What if I don't like condoms?
There probably isn't a person in the world who actually prefers sex with a condom to sex without. Some guys complain that their penis doesn't feel quite as sensitive with a condom, and not many people particularly like stopping whatever they're doing to put a condom on. But any intelligent person should realise that there's no choice. It would be a lovely feeling if you could go scuba diving without having to wear goggles and an oxygen tank, but no one would try it, because wearing diving gear is a

far better option than drowning, isn't it? The same goes for condoms. They're not that much hassle, they don't make that much difference to how sex feels (most people find they make no difference at all) and using one is a tiny price to pay for peace of mind. When you're wearing a condom, you can just relax and enjoy yourself – what could be better than that?

What happens if I get into a situation where I wasn't expecting to have sex, and we don't have any condoms?
Don't have sex! You could always snog, cuddle or even masturbate each other instead.

If you feel like you might get carried away, though, and not be able to resist the lure of actual sex, then do something else entirely – watch telly, eat something, go for a walk, whatever. Then make a date for tomorrow night that you can both look forward to – and decide who's going to bring the condoms!

Remember: if you always carry a condom, you'll never get into that situation!

What about using condoms for oral sex?
Oral sex is licking, kissing, or sucking someone's private parts. Yes, in order to minimise the risk of STIs, sexual health experts recommend using condoms for oral sex on guys. For oral sex on girls, it's recommended that you use a latex square, or 'dental dam', which is available free from sexual health clinics.

Can you re-use a condom?
No. Condoms are designed to be chucked out after one use. Never re-use them.

How do condoms protect against STIs?
Condoms protect against STIs because they create a barrier between the vagina and the penis which keeps each person's *secretions* separate. Secretions are the wetness produced by

and on female and male private parts – such as the mucus within the vagina and the semen that comes from the penis. Without the protection of a condom, these secretions can enter your bloodstream through small cuts and tears on the skin of your genitals and cause STIs. Spermicide used to coat condoms also acts against STIs – in particular, a spermicide called Nonoxynol-9, which kills the HIV virus, and some other STI germs.

Is there any time when it's safe to have sex without using a condom or a female condom?
There are some circumstances where you could be pretty sure that you weren't at risk from STIs. Even so, you wouldn't be safe from the risk of pregnancy. If you don't wear a condom or a female condom, and you don't want to make a baby, you'll need to use some other form of contraception. These are the circumstances where you wouldn't need to worry about STIs and so might not have to use condoms:

• If you and your partner are both virgins, and have never shared a needle for drugs. This means you don't have to worry about passing sexually transmitted infections on to each other. However, you have to be 100% sure that your partner is telling the truth about their history. It's really a question of trust, and you could actually be trusting your partner with your life – so you'd have to be really certain.

• If you and your partner have both been through tests for STIs which proved negative – as long as neither of you had slept (or shared a needle) with anyone else for at least three months before you had the test or slept (or shared a needle) with anyone else since. Many people in steady relationships who plan to stay together for a long time in the future take STI tests so that they can stop using condoms.

The condom is the only form of contraception that protects

against pregnancy and most STIs, but there are other types of contraception available, which protect only against pregnancy.

Except for the Emergency Contraceptive Pill, which you can sometimes buy from a pharmacy, the contraceptives listed all have to be prescribed by a doctor or a nurse, so you will need to get them from a young person's clinic, your GP or a family planning clinic. The health practitioner there will ask you questions about your medical history and, if you're considering a hormonal contraceptive, they will also need to know about your family's medical history and will take your blood pressure and weigh you. All of this is to check which contraceptive will suit you best.

To make the list of contraceptives easier for you to digest, we've grouped them together according to things they have in common.

Hormonal Methods of Contraception

The following three methods all use the hormones oestrogen and progestogen to prevent pregnancy.

The Combined Pill

. . . comes in packets of twenty-one tablets, which you take every day until you finish one pack. Then you have a seven-day break, where you will probably have a light 'withdrawal bleed'. After this, you start taking a new pack. If you take it more than twenty-four hours late and if you experience vomiting or diarrhoea, you will need to use another form of contraceptive, like a condom, to provide protection during this time.

The Contraceptive Patch

. . . also called Evra, is a small beige patch that you stick on your skin like a sticky plaster, where it releases hormones into your bloodstream through the skin. You wear it continuously for seven days (it's very sticky, so you can even swim in it), and on the eighth day you take it off and throw it away, replacing it with a new one. After three weeks you don't wear the patch for seven days, when you may have a withdrawal bleed. Then you start a four-week cycle again with a new patch.

The Vaginal Ring

. . . aka Nuvaring, is a fairly new method of contraception. As the name implies, it's a soft, plastic ring that goes into your vagina, where it slowly releases hormones. Once in place, the ring should mould itself to your body and stay there. You leave it in your vagina, continuously, for three weeks. Then you take it out and have seven ring-free days, when you will have light withdrawal bleeding. At the end of this week, you insert a new ring and begin the four-week cycle again.

How they all work

These three methods of contraception all use the same two hormones to prevent pregnancy. These are oestrogen and progestogen. These hormones work by stopping *ovulation* (the release of eggs) and by thickening the mucus around the cervix (the neck of the womb), which makes it difficult for sperm to get through and into the womb. They also make the lining of the womb thinner, so that a fertilised egg can't implant there. All this makes these three methods of contraception very efficient – 99% effective – which means that one in a hundred who use them properly will get pregnant each year.

NB: Unless you start using them at the beginning of your menstrual cycle you will need to use an alternative method of contraception (ie, a condom) for up to seven days.

Disadvantages:
• They don't protect against STIs – always use a condom for this.
• The use of some prescription medicines, including some antibiotics, medicines used to treat epilepsy, HIV and TB, and the complementary medicine St John's Wort, can all make these types of contraception less effective, and they will not be prescribed to you if you have ever suffered from severe migraines or have high blood pressure or bleeding between periods.
• Side effects can include headaches, feeling sick, mood swings, sore boobs, and weight gain or loss. However, these should stop within a few months.

Advantages:
• None of the three methods interrupt sex (even the vaginal ring, apparently!).
• They can make your periods more regular, lighter and less painful, and you'll be less likely to suffer from PMS (premenstrual syndrome).
• They can help reduce spotty skin.

The following three contraceptive methods use only one hormone, progestogen, to prevent pregnancy.

The Progestogen Only Pill (POP or Mini Pill)

... comes in a packet of twenty-eight small pills, one of which you take every day, at exactly the same time. Choose a time of day that's convenient for you. When you've finished the pack, start a new one straight away. You will need to use a condom as an extra precaution if you have vomiting or diarrhoea.

The Contraceptive Injection.

There are two types – Depo-Provera, which gives twelve weeks' protection against pregnancy, and Noristerat, which give eight weeks' protection. A doctor or nurse injects the contraceptive into a muscle, usually in your arm or bottom.

The Contraceptive Implant

. . . is a small, flexible tube about the size of a matchstick. It is placed under the skin in your upper arm by a doctor or nurse, where it slowly releases progestogen. You will be given a local anaesthetic to numb the skin first, and it should only take a few minutes to insert. You won't need stitches. Once it's in, it protects against pregnancy for three years.

How they all work:

The progestogen they contain makes the mucus around the cervix thicker, so that sperm find it difficult to pass through into the womb. The hormone also thins the womb-lining, making it difficult for a fertilised egg to implant there. In some women it also stops ovulation. All are very effective at preventing pregnancy – over 99%, which means that less than one in a hundred women who use the methods properly will get pregnant each year.

NB Depending on when you start using these forms of contraception, you may need to use extra protection (ie condoms) for up to seven days initially.

Disadvantages:

• The use of some prescription medicines, such as antibiotics and medicines to treat epilepsy, HIV and TB, and the complementary medicine, St John's Wort, can make them less effective.

• They don't protect against STIs – use a condom for this.

• Some girls get spotty skin, sore boobs, mood swings and

headaches for the first few months of using them.

• Your periods may become irregular – they may happen more often, less often, be lighter or stop altogether.

Advantanges:

• They don't interrupt sex.

• They can be used by girls who can't use contraceptive methods that include oestrogen (the combined pill, the contraceptive patch and the vaginal ring).

Intrauterine Devices

The IUS (Intrauterine system, or the Mirena)

. . . is a small piece of T-shaped plastic, about 3cm long, which is fitted into the uterus (womb). It has one or two threads attached to it, which hang down from the neck of the womb (so you can check it's in place). The IUS contains the hormone progestogen, which works to prevent pregnancy by thickening the mucus in your cervix and thinning the womb lining. It also sometimes stops ovulation. In fact, your periods will probably become lighter and period pain often disappears. Once in place, the IUS can prevent pregnancy for up to five years. It's more than 99% effective in preventing pregnancy – that means that less than one in a hundred women who use an IUS will get pregnant every year.

The IUD (the intrauterine device, or the coil)

. . . is about the same size as the IUS, but comes in several shapes, and is made of copper or plastic. Like the IUS, it is fitted into the uterus and has one or two threads attached which hang through the cervix so you can check it's in place. The IUD works by killing sperm before they can get to an egg, and by stopping eggs implanting in the womb. It can prevent pregnancy for five to ten years, depending on the device. The IUD is 98-99% effective at preventing pregnancy – which means that between one and two women in a hundred who use an IUD will get pregnant each year.

How are the IUS and the IUD put in?
A trained doctor or nurse will fit your IUS or IUD. They're put into the uterus through your vagina, which takes fifteen to twenty minutes. It can be uncomfortable or painful for some women, so you'll be offered painkillers. You may also have some period-type pain and light bleeding for a few days after the IUS or IUD has been inserted.

You'll be protected from pregnancy as soon as the IUS or IUD has been fitted. Once it's in place, you'll need to go back for a check-up three to six weeks later, when the doctor or nurse will check that it's still in place, and show you how to check it yourself. You do this by feeling for the threads that hang from it down the neck of the womb. You'll need to check yourself every month after that, and go back to the clinic if there are any changes.

Disadvantages:
• If the IUS or the IUD move out of place they'll be less effective.
• They don't protect against STIs. You need to use a condom to protect against STIs.
• They can be painful to fit in place.
• The IUS can cause irregular bleeding at first and temporary side effects such as tender boobs and skin problems.
• The IUD can cause heavier, more painful and longer lasting periods.
• If the IUD fails, there is a risk that pregnancy might happen in the fallopian tube. This is known as an ectopic pregnancy, and it can cause very serious health problems.

Advantages:
- They don't interrupt sex.
- They work immediately when they've been fitted and they're easily removed if you no longer want them.
- Your fertility (ability to have babies) will go back to normal as soon as the device is removed.
- They're not affected by other medicines, and there are no side effects.

Diaphragms and Caps with Spermicide

Diaphragms (pronounced *die-a-fram*) and cervical caps are thin, circular domes with a flexible rim, made of rubber or silicone. They both fit into the vagina and go over the cervix (the neck of the womb), preventing sperm from entering the womb. Because women's cervixes vary in size, diaphragms and caps come in different sizes too, and they'll be specially fitted to suit you by a nurse or a doctor. They're both always used together with spermicide.

A diaphragm or cap with spermicide can go in any time before sex. But if you put one in more than three hours before you have sex, you need to reach up your vagina and put extra spermicide around it to be safe.

The doctor or nurse who fit the diaphragm or cap will explain in detail how to insert and remove them, and will help you to do so in the clinic.

Diaphragms and caps with spermicide are 92-96% effective if used properly. This means that four to eight women in every hundred who use the cap will get pregnant each year. They must be left in for at least six hours after sex to be effective, and you need to add more spermicide if you have sex again.

Disadvantages:
- If you gain or lose weight, you may need to get a different size fitted.

• They don't protect you against STIs – use a condom for this.

• It can take a little while before you're confident about using them, and not all women are comfortable with putting them in.

• Some diaphragm users get frequent bouts of cystitis (see page 126) – changing to a cap might help.

• They can't be used by women who are allergic to latex rubber or spermicide, and you can't use oil-based lubricants with them either. All that spermicide can feel wet and messy to you and your partner!

Advantages:

• You only need to use them when you have sex, and they can be put in before sex so they don't disturb the moment.

• They're not affected by any medicines.

• You and your partner can't feel them when you have sex.

• They don't disturb your periods – in fact, you can use them as sanitary protection during your period – they will collect the blood!

Emergency Contraception

Emergency contraception can be used up to five days after sex to prevent pregnancy if other methods of contraception have failed: for instance, if a condom splits or a pill is forgotten, or taken late, or if no contraception is used. There are two forms of emergency contraception: the Emergency Contraceptive Pill (sometimes called the 'EC Pill' or the 'morning after pill'), and the Emergency Interuterine Device (IUD).

The Emergency Contraceptive Pill (EC pill)

The important thing to remember about the EC pill is that it's not meant for regular use. Although there are no long-term risks to taking it, it's essential to use another, regular method of contraception before you have sex next time. Other methods are more readily available, have fewer side-effects and protect you against pregnancy all of the time.

There are two types of Emergency Contraceptive Pills, and they both work by using the hormone progestogen to stop the release of an egg, or, if an egg has been fertilised, by stopping it settling into the wall of your womb. You can get the EC pill at some pharmacies (as long as you're over sixteen), as well as at family planning clinics, sexual health clinics, NHS walk-in clinics, some A and E departments, Brook Centres and your GPs (not in Jersey). It's available free of charge, unless you get it from a pharmacy, where it costs about £25. The health practitioners or pharmacist will need to ask you one or two questions about your health and what medication you're on before giving you the pills.

The two types of EC pill are Levonelle and ellaOne. Despite their sometimes being called the 'morning after pill', Levonelle can be taken up to three days following unprotected sex and ellaOne can be taken up to five days later. ellaOne, because it's very new, is only available with a prescription and is not always easy to get hold of. For this reason, the following details are about Levonelle. Levonelle comes in packs of one or two pills, which you need to take as soon as possible after unprotected sex. Remember that the emergency contraceptive pill is more effective the sooner you take it. When you take it within twenty four hours of unprotected sex, it's 95% effective at preventing pregnancy. When you take it between twenty-five to forty-eight hours after it's 85% effective, and when it's taken between forty-nine to seventy-two hours after it's 58% effective. So it's very important that you get advice on emergency contraception as soon as possible after unprotected sex.

Disadvantages:

• If you throw up within two hours of taking the pill or pills, it can be less effective. If this happens, talk to the doctor, nurse or pharmacist who gave it to you – they may give you more or suggest you have an IUD fitted.

• The pill is less effective if you have had unprotected sex at another time – either since you had your last period or since you took the emergency pill.

• Some prescribed medicines and complementary medicines such as St John's Wort affect the EC pill, and you may need to take a higher dose if this is the case.

• Some girls experience some short-term side effects, such as feeling a bit sick, dizzy or tired after taking it. You might also have headaches, sore breasts and tummy pain. People occasionally throw up.

• You won't know for sure that it's worked until you start your period.

Advantages:

• If you've had unprotected sex or your contraception failed, taking it means that you're very unlikely to get pregnant.

• Almost anyone can use it, it doesn't have long-term or serious health risks, and it's safe to take more than once a month, if necessary.

The Emergency Intrauterine Device (IUD)

The Emergency Intrauterine Device is a small, T-shaped piece of plastic and copper, which is inserted into the womb through the vagina. It's just the same as the IUD described on page 103, and it can be fitted up to five days after you've had unprotected sex. It works both by stopping eggs from being fertilised by sperm and by stopping fertilised eggs from implanting in the womb.

You can get the emergency IUD fitted at a Brook centre, a family planning clinic or a sexual health (GUM) clinic. It's best to ring the clinic or surgery first to check that there's someone there trained to fit one.

You need to go back to see the doctor or nurse who fitted it three or four weeks later, whether you've had your period or not, to make sure you're not pregnant. The IUD can be removed after your period has arrived, or kept in as a regular method of contraception.

Disadvantages:
• There's a very small chance of getting an infection in your womb within the first twenty days of it being put in, and sometimes the IUD can be pushed out by your womb. If either of these things happen, speak to a nurse or doctor.

Advantages:
• It's almost 100% effective against pregnancy, provided it's fitted within five days of unprotected sex taking place.
• It's are not affected by other medicines, doesn't have side effects, and is suitable for most women.

Now You're All Clued-up . . .

Phew! After digesting all this information about contraception you should have plenty of ideas about what might be good for you, and what might not. Sadly, as you can see, there's no perfect method of birth control – they all have their drawbacks, and none of them can provide 100% protection against pregnancy, or against STIs. But now you're a pretty well-informed individual and you're on the way to making the best and safest contraceptive choice for you.

Remember that if you and your partner don't get on with one method, you can always try another. Your GP or a doctor or nurse at your nearest Family Planning Clinic or Brook centre will be able to tell you even more about birth control and supply you with what you need.

Chapter 6

Sexually Transmitted Infections (STIs)

Ideally, everyone's sexual experiences will be happy and healthy. Unfortunately, this isn't always the case. Sexually transmitted infections are on the rise in this country, particularly among teenagers. This means that the risk of getting an STI is something that you have to consider and prepare for *every* time you have sex. This chapter is all about the sorts of diseases and infections you can pick up through having sex, or having close sexual contact, with another person. In it, you'll find:

- STIs – What's the Deal?
- Virgins Can Have STIs Too
- Where to Get Checked Out For STIs
- What to Look For With STIs
- What If My Tests Show I Have an STI?
- Types of Sexually Transmitted Infections
- Developing Your Sense of Self-preservation

STIs –
What's the Deal?

You can't tell whether someone has an STI by looking at them. Many STIs don't show symptoms, so a person may have a disease that they pass on to you without knowing about it, and vice versa.

It's very important to be checked out and treated for STIs as soon as possible, because if left untreated, STIs can cause you and your partners serious problems. This goes for women especially – if you have an untreated STI, you may find it difficult, or even impossible, to have a baby in the future.

This is the reason why it's essential to use a condom every time you have sex, even if you are using another method of contraception, like the pill. You can even catch some things if you *are* using a condom, so it's definitely worth knowing what you're up against. It's also essential, when you meet a new partner, for both of you to get tested at a clinic before anything sexual happens, to make sure that nothing passes between you.

Virgins Can Have STIs Too . . .

You don't have to have penetrative sex (where the penis enters the vagina) to catch STIs. Some STIs, such as genital herpes and genital warts, can be passed on by touching each others' private parts, and by oral sex. So it's important to get checked out if you've ever been this intimate with anyone, even if you're technically a virgin.

Even if you've never had *any* kind of sexual contact with

another person, don't skip this chapter! It's very important to know about STIs so that if and when you're ready to start having sex, you'll know how to protect yourself and your partner.

Where to Get Checked Out for STIs

If you think you have an infection, or if you and your partner are thinking of starting a sexual relationship, you need to visit a clinic as soon as possible. Get tested quickly! It's very easy, and the sooner you go, the sooner you can set your mind to rest. You can go to your GP, but generally STIs are diagnosed and treated in sexual health clinics, also known as genito-urinary medicine (GUM) clinics. Contact Ask Brook on 0808 802 1234 to find your nearest clinic, or look online at www.nhs.uk under 'sexual health services' or find them in the phone book under GUM or Sexual Health.

What happens at a sexual health (GUM) clinic?
Staff at sexual health clinics are friendly and professional, and they won't judge you. All services at these clinics is confidential – that means that they won't tell anyone that you have visited or what you came for. You can go to any clinic you want – it doesn't have to be your local one. Plus, you don't have to give your real name or any details about yourself if you don't want to. You don't need an appointment to go there, or a referral from your GP (you don't even need to tell your GP you're going) and the whole thing is free. All in all, a visit to an STD clinic is not the big deal you might

fear, so there is no excuse for not going.

A routine check-up tests for chlamydia, gonorrhoea, trichomonas vaginalis and syphilis (see below for more details on all these conditions). You'll be asked what type of sex (eg, vaginal sex, oral sex, anal sex) you've been having and with whom, and whether you have any symptoms which may need further tests.

If you are getting tested for HIV because you are worried that you may have been at risk, you'll usually be offered some counselling before the test. This is to help you prepare for how you may feel and react if the test result is positive.

The clinic will contact you within a few days, usually by phone or text, to let you know the results of the tests. If they phone they make sure that they deliver the results to the right person, and they word their side of the conversation so that anyone listening won't realise what you're discussing. If there's anything that needs treatment, the clinic will ask you to come back.

It's easy to diagnose and treat most STIs, so if you are even slightly worried that you have one, go straight to your local sexual health clinic.

What to Look for with STIs

Although you may have an STI and show no symptoms at all, here's a list of things to look out for:
- pain or burning when weeing
- sore genitals
- pain during sex
- weeing more often than usual
- unusual discharge from the vagina or penis, perhaps smelly, thick, yellow, white or cloudy

• rashes, itching, blisters sores or lumps on or near the genitals
• for girls, bleeding after sex or between periods

What If My Tests Show I Have an STI?

The first thing to do is to try not to worry. Most STIs are easily treatable with antibiotics. If you test positive for any STI, your clinic will treat the condition, and will encourage you to talk to your current partner and sometimes to your previous partners, so that they can be tested too. The staff at the clinic know that this can be difficult and will help you find the best way to do it.

If you really don't want to tell your partner or your former partners yourself, they can do this for you, without even mentioning your name.

Types of STIs

There are over 25 STIs, but here are the most common ones:

Chlamydia

Chlamydia is caused by a type of bacteria that is passed to others through semen and vaginal fluid. It's one of the most common STIs in the UK, and it's on the increase, particularly amongst teenagers. It's a tricky STI, because most people who have it show no symptoms, and may go on to infect others unknowingly. Untreated, it can spread to other parts of your body, causing pain and inflammation in the joints in both boys and girls. In addition, women are at risk of developing PID – pelvic inflammatory disease – which can lead to infertility in the future.

However, the good news about chlamydia is that it's very easy to diagnose and to treat.

How is chlamydia passed on?
Through unprotected (ie, without a condom) vaginal sex, oral sex or anal sex.

How to recognise chlamydia
Half of infected men and 80% of infected women show no symptoms at all. Here are some of the signs of chlamydia for those who do show symptoms.
Girls: unusual vaginal discharge; pain when weeing; heavy periods or bleeding between periods; lower tummy pain; tummy pain during vaginal sex; bleeding during or after sex.
Boys: white/cloudy and watery discharge from the penis; pain when weeing; painful swelling of testicles.

Tests and treatment for chlamydia
A doctor or nurse will take a swab. This is a very simple and painless procedure – a thing like a large cotton bud is used to gently wipe the affected area (usually the cervix or the tip of the penis) to collect some of the mucus there. A urine sample may also be taken. Chlamydia is really easy to treat – usually with a single dose of antibiotics. Don't have sex or drink alcohol until treatment is complete (alcohol and antibiotics don't mix).
It's also possible to get postal testing kits in some parts of the UK, which involve sending a urine sample or a swab through

the post to be screened. You can find out if this is available in your area by visiting the National Chlamydia Screening webside (www.chlamydiascreening.nhs.uk).

Protecting against chlamydia
Use condoms whenever you have sex, including oral sex. Latex squares, or dental dams, available from sexual health clinics, should be used for oral sex on a girl.

Genital Herpes
Genital herpes is a viral infection caused by the herpes simplex virus. There are two types of this virus – herpes simplex 1 and herpes simplex 2. These days, the two viruses can both cause outbreaks of facial herpes (cold sores), herpes on the fingers (whitlows) and genital herpes (sores on or around the genitals). People with herpes usually have an initial outbreak of itchy, painful sores which tend to disappear as the virus becomes inactive in their body for a while, before becoming active again and causing further outbreaks.

The herpes virus is very common – six out of ten people in the UK have either herpes simplex one or two (or both) by the age of twenty five.

How is genital herpes passed on?
You can catch genital herpes by:

1) having vaginal or anal sex with someone who has genital herpes,

2) being given oral sex by someone with facial herpes (cold sores), or

3) being touched around the genitals by a person with herpes (whitlows) on their fingers. The herpes virus is at its most infectious just before, during or just after an outbreak, when blisters or sores are present. You can't spread the virus to

other parts of your own body, and it will only reappear at or close to the same site – eg herpes caught on your lip won't recur on your chin.

How to recognise genital herpes

If you've been in contact with the virus, symptoms usually appear within two to seven days. These are: tingling or itching on or around the genital area followed by the appearance of small, painful blisters. With the initial infection, some people feel as if they are coming down with the flu – with headache, backache, temperature and burning sensation when weeing. Most people only have one or two outbreaks of genital herpes, but some may have more regular recurrences.

However, lots of people who have the virus don't show any symptoms, and are unaware that they carry it.

Tests and treatment for genital herpes

Herpes can only be diagnosed when someone is showing signs of the virus – ie, they have blisters or sores. Testing is done by taking a swab from the infected area.

As yet there is no cure for genital herpes, but an anti-viral drug can reduce the severity of outbreaks.

If you think you or your partner have genital herpes, it's important to get it diagnosed, so that you can avoid sexual contact while sores are present.

Protecting against genital herpes

Condoms can protect against genital herpes, but it depends where the sores are. For example, if a boy has blisters on his penis, a condom will protect his girlfriend as long as all his blisters are covered. But if a girl has sores around the outside of her vagina, a condom will not provide enough coverage to protect her boyfriend. Whoever diagnoses you will be able to suggest ways to have safe sex. For more information, ring the

Herpes Virus Association Helpline on 0845 123 2305 or visit their website at www.herpes.org.uk.

Genital Warts

Genital warts are the most common STI. They are caused by the human papilloma virus (HPV or wart virus) and occur on skin on and around the genitals. Other warts on the body (such as those you get on your hands, or veruccas on your feet) are caused by different types of the HPV virus.

How are genital warts passed on?
The genital wart virus is easily passed from an infected person to another through unprotected vaginal sex, anal sex and oral sex. It can also be passed on through skin to skin contact.

How to recognise genital warts
Warts can take from two weeks to a year or more to develop after infection with the wart virus, and they can occur anywhere in the genital area of boys and girls. A person can pass the virus on without having any visible warts themselves. Or they may have tiny warts that they have not noticed, or warts that are invisible because they occur inside the vagina – particularly on the cervix (the neck of the womb) – or in the anus (bottom). Boys can also have warts inside their penises that they are unaware of.

Genital warts are usually painless and range in size from so tiny they can't be seen to the size of the end of a pencil. They come on their own and in groups.

Tests and treatment for genital warts
Doctors sometimes wipe the area with vinegar which makes the warts turn white so that they are more visible. Warts can be treated by painting on chemical ointments or chemical

paints, by freezing or surgical removal under local anaesthetic.

There's no treatment to get rid of the wart virus completely. Once you have the wart virus, warts are likely to appear at some point. Untreated warts sometimes go away on their own. Some people's warts may take some time, despite treatment, to disappear completely. Some warts don't reappear after the first episode, but others keep returning.

If you suspect you or your partner have genital warts, you must get them diagnosed and treated. If you don't, they may grow in size and multiply, and you risk passing them on to others.

Protecting against genital warts

Although condoms protect against most STIs, they are not 100% effective in preventing the transmission of the genital wart virus – especially if the warts are outside the area the condom covers. Sexual health experts advise that you avoid sex until warts have been successfully treated, and that you seek help if you think you have caught the virus.

Gonorrhoea

Gonorrhoea (also known as *the clap*, *drip* or *sting*) is a bacterial infection, like chlamydia, but less common. Left untreated gonorrhoea can lead to serious health problems: infertility (inability to have babies) and inflammation of the joints or the eyes.

How is gonorrhoea passed on?

Through unprotected sex, including oral sex.

How to recognise gonorrhoea

About 10% of men and 50% of women will not have obvious signs of gonorrhoea. If you do get symptoms, they appear one to fourteen days after infection, and sometimes months later.

Girls: thin white, yellow or green discharge from the vagina; needing to wee frequently; pain when weeing; rarely, lower stomach pain; heavier than usual periods, or bleeding between periods.

Boys: thin white, yellow or green discharge from the penis; pain when weeing; painful testicles.

Tests and treatments for gonorrhoea

A doctor or nurse will take swabs from the infected areas and possibly a urine sample. Gonorrhoea is easily cured by antibiotics.

How to protect against gonorrhoea

Use condoms whenever you have sex, including oral sex. For oral sex on a girl, use dental dams – latex squares available from sexual health clinics.

Hepatitis B

Hepatitis B is caused by the hepatitis B virus. It's very infectious and although it's not that common, it isn't rare. It can lead to serious liver disease, and liver cancer.

How is hepatitis B passed on?

By unprotected sex, contact with blood or blood-stained saliva and urine.

How to recognise hepatitis B

Many people have no symptoms, so may not know that they are carrying the virus. Others may experience flu-like symptoms and jaundice, where the whites of their eyes and their skin turn yellow.

Tests and treatments for hepatitis B

A blood test shows whether you have the virus. There's no treatment available for the infection, and although most people recover completely after rest, some may end up with long-term liver damage. You can get vaccinated against hepatitis B at sexual health clinics.

How to protect against hepatitis B

Use condoms whenever you have sex or oral sex. Use dental dams (latex squares available from sexual health clinics) for oral sex on girls. As it's such an infectious virus, you can also catch it from kissing and sharing toothbrushes and drinks.

HIV and AIDS

HIV stands for Human Immunodeficiency Virus. There are an estimated 86,500 people living with HIV in the UK, and a quarter of them are so far unaware of their infection. HIV is a virus that damages the body's immune system so that it can no longer fight off infections. HIV can lead to AIDS (Acquired Immune Deficiency Syndrome). AIDS is the name for the collection of illnesses that people get when their immune system has been damaged in this way. Because anti-HIV drug treatments are now available that slow the damage the virus does, people with HIV are living much longer and feeling much healthier than they did fifteen or so years ago. However, there's still no cure for HIV, it's still considered a fatal disease, and it's still not clear what the long-term situation will be for those with the virus. Therefore it's very, very important to prevent the spread of HIV by using condoms whenever you have sex. In the past, the virus was mainly transmitted between men who had sex with men, but these days the amount of heterosexuals with HIV outnumbers homosexuals. And around one in ten new HIV cases are in young people aged sixteen to twenty-four.

How is HIV passed on?

The virus is mostly passed on through sex without a condom. Bodily fluids containing enough virus to infect someone are blood (including period blood), vaginal fluids, semen and breast milk. Drug users who share needles can pass on the virus, and a pregnant mother with HIV can pass on the virus during pregnancy or after the birth through breast-feeding. HIV is *not* transmitted by everyday social contact. This means you can't get HIV from shaking hands, kissing, sharing toilet seats, cutlery, going to swimming pools or from having your food prepared by someone who is HIV positive.

How to recognise HIV/AIDS

When someone is first infected with the HIV virus, they may get a high temperature, swollen glands and night sweats. After that, there's usually a long period – up to 10 years or more – when they have no symptoms. But without treatment from anti-HIV drugs, their immune system will gradually weaken from the effort of fighting the virus. Then they are likely to get an infection, like pneumonia, that they can't fight off.

Tests and treatments for HIV/AIDS

A doctor or nurse will take a sample of blood. You can't be tested for HIV until you've been infected for at least three months, as it takes this long for evidence of the virus to appear in your blood. However, you could still pass on the virus to someone else during this three-month period.

There's no cure for HIV. Current treatment consists of a combination of three or more antiviral drugs that must be taken every day for life. These can help slow the damage that the virus does to the immune system, and so prolong the life of those with HIV. It's still not clear what will happen to people with the virus in the long term – specialists reckon that their life expectancy will probably be reduced. Once a person has the HIV virus, they will always be infectious.

How to protect against HIV
Use condoms whenever you have sex. Although there's only a small risk of getting HIV through oral sex, it's best to play safe and use condoms and dental dams (latex squares available from sexual health clinics for use on girls) for oral sex.

Non-Specific Genital Infections (NSGIs)
This is a large group of infections of the genitals that includes:
- Vaginitis (inflammation of the vagina)
- Urethritis (inflammation of the urethra – or wee hole)
- Cystitis (inflammation of the bladder)
- Proctitis (inflammation of the rectum – or bottom)

How are NSGIs passed on?
Some NSGIs, like cystitis, are not necessarily passed on by sexual contact. Some may be caused by chlamydia, especially in men.

How to recognise NSGIs
Symptoms of NSGIs include: discharge from the vagina, urethra (wee hole) or anus (bottom); inflammation of the genital area; pain or burning sensations when weeing; sore or swollen genitals.

Tests and treatment for NSGIs
A doctor or nurse would usually take a swab from the infected area, and/or ask for a urine sample. Treatment is usually by antibiotics. Remember not to drink alcohol when you take antibiotics for anything.

How to protect against NSGIs
Use a condom for sex, including oral sex. Dental dams (latex squares available from sexual health clinics) should be used for oral sex on a girl.

A Word About Cystitis
Cystitis is a very common NSGI, particularly for girls – at least half of all women get it at some point. Boys can get it as well, but not in such large numbers. It's an infection of the bladder which is caused mainly by bacteria that normally live in your bottom and can easily be spread to your urethra (wee hole) and up to your bladder. It can also be caused by the friction of having lots of penetrative sex. The condition is not sexually transmitted however.

How to recognise cystitis
Wanting to wee very often, and feeling as if you're bursting to go; burning or pain when weeing; unusual urine that may smell different or look cloudy or contain blood. Some women get a high temperature and/or tummy pain.

Tests and treatment for cystitis
A doctor or nurse can often diagnose cystitis from the symptoms, but they may ask for a specimen of urine too. It's often treated with antibiotics, but once you've had it and know the symptoms, you can treat it yourself with cystitis remedies you can buy from supermarkets and chemists. Drinking lots of water and cranberry juice can help get rid of it too. If you are prescribed antibiotics, don't drink alcohol while you're taking them.

How to protect against cystitis
Drink plenty of water – at least one and a half litres a day.

Always try to wee after sex to flush any germs out of your bladder, and always wipe yourself from front to back when you've been to the loo to avoid spreading germs from your bottom to your urethra.

Pubic Lice (Crabs)

Pubic lice, also known as crabs, are tiny (2mm long), yellowy-grey crab-like creatures which live in the pubic hair. If they are left untreated, the lice may occasionally spread to other parts of the body, including chest hair and eyelashes. Pubic lice live on human blood but can survive for twenty four hours off the body.

How are pubic lice passed on?

Pubic lice can be sexually transmitted, but can also be passed on through close body contact, or by just sharing towels and bed linen.

How to recognise pubic lice

Pubic lice are so small that they're difficult to see, so you may not notice them at all. You may see other signs like: itching in the affected areas; black, powdery droppings from the lice in your underwear; brown eggs on pubic or other body hair; irritation and inflammation in the affected area, sometimes caused by scratching; sky-blue spots (which disappear within a few days) or very tiny specks of blood on the skin.

Tests and treatment for pubic lice

The doctor or nurse may use a magnifying glass to check for the lice and eggs. Pubic lice won't go away on their own – treatment is a lotion, cream or shampoos.

How to protect against pubic lice
Condoms don't protect against pubic lice. If you think you or your partner might have them, you should both go for a check-up. Until you've had the all-clear, don't have sex with or share towels, bedding or clothes with anyone.

Scabies
Scabies is caused by a very tiny (0.4mm long) mite called Sarcoptes scabei. These mites can be found in the genital area, on the hands, between the fingers, on the wrists and elbows, underneath the arms, on the tummy, on the breasts, around the nipples in women, on the feet and ankles, and around the buttocks – pretty much all over, in fact! The mites burrow into skin and lay their eggs, which can cause terrible itching.

How is scabies passed on?
Scabies is passed on easily through close body contact, sexual or non-sexual. Because scabies mites can live for up to seventy two hours away from the body, they can survive for this long on bedding, clothes and towels and be passed on in that way too.

How to recognise scabies
The mites themselves are too small for you to see. You may not get any symptoms, or you may experience the following: intense itching in the infected areas that gets worse at night; an itchy red rash or tiny spots (the rash can look like other itchy conditions, such as eczema); inflammation or raw, broken skin in the affected areas, usually caused by scratching.

Tests and treatment for scabies
The doctor or nurse can often tell just by looking at the affected areas, or they may take a flake of skin from a spot to check under a microscope for the mites. Treatment is with a

special lotion or cream and usually does the trick. You will also want to wash all bedding, towels and clothing to avoid reinfection. Scabies won't go away on its own.

How to protect against scabies
Condoms don't protect against scabies. If you think you or your partner might have it, you should both go for a check-up immediately. Don't have any sexual contact, sleep in the same bed or share clothes, towels, etc, until you've both had the all-clear.

Syphilis

Syphilis (the pox) is a bacterial, sexually transmitted infection. It's less common than some other STIs but, worryingly, it's on the rise in the UK. Left untreated, syphilis can cause very serious damage to the heart, brain, lungs, eyes and other organs, which can be fatal. If it's contracted in pregnancy it can cause stillbirth or congenital infection – which means that the baby will be born infected by syphilis.

How is syphilis passed on?
Through unprotected sex, including oral sex, or through close body contact with someone who has syphilis sores or rashes.

How to recognise syphilis
Because the symptoms of syphilis can be very mild, people may not know they have it and could pass it on to others without realising. Symptoms usually take this course: three to four weeks after coming into contact with the disease, you get sores around your genital area or sometimes your mouth or anus, which take several weeks to heal. If untreated, this is followed by a rash all over your body or in patches, flu-like symptoms and tiredness. Symptoms can then vanish, but the

disease is still there and you remain infectious.

Tests and treatment for syphilis

A doctor or nurse will take a blood sample and sometimes a urine sample and swabs from sores. Treatment is by antibiotics and is very effective. Remember not to drink alcohol when you take antibiotics for anything.

Protecting against syphilis

Use condoms whenever you have sex. For oral sex, use condoms on boys, and dental dams (latex squares available from sexual health clinics) on girls.

Thrush (Candidiasis)

Thrush is caused by a kind of yeast, Candida albicans. Normally, this yeast lives harmlessly inside the vagina but sometimes the amount of yeast increases and this causes thrush. It's very common for girls to get thrush – three out of four women will get it at some point in their lives, and some get it regularly. Men sometimes get it too.

How is thrush passed on?

Thrush isn't caused by sexual contact, though it can be passed on this way. It can be triggered by several things: the use of antibiotics and some forms of the contraceptive pill; strongly-scented bath or shower products and body sprays; being run-down and stressed out; wearing tight underwear or trousers made from synthetic material like nylon.

How to recognise thrush

Some people get no symptoms, and girls with the condition are more likely to show symptoms than boys.

Girls: a thick, white vaginal discharge (like cottage cheese); itching; soreness; swelling of the vulva (the lips of the vagina); pain when weeing.

Boys: a sore, itchy and inflamed penis; white cottage-cheeselike discharge under the foreskin.

Tests and treatment for thrush

A doctor or nurse will take a swab from the affected area and might ask for a urine sample. Thrush is treated with anti-fungal pills, creams and vaginal pessaries. A pessary is a kind of pill that you insert into your vagina with a plastic applicator. You *can* buy pessaries and cream yourself from the chemists', but it's always best to get a diagnosis from a health practitioner first; because lots of other infections can have similar symptoms.

Protecting against thrush

A condom stops the condition being passed on – always wear one for sex. Try not to use perfumed soap and other scented products on your genitals – use unperfumed products, or just plain water to wash yourself. Nylon knickers can make the condition worse – cotton ones are much better as they let the air flow through! Girls – use pads instead of tampons when you have your period, and wipe yourself from front to back when you've been to the loo – so that bacteria from your bottom don't come in contact with your vaginal area.

Trichomoniasis (TV)

Trichomoniasis, also known as Trichomonas Vaginalis or TV, is caused by tiny parasites infecting the vagina in women and the urethra (wee hole) in both men and women. In itself it's not that serious a condition, but it's often diagnosed alongside gonorrhoea, which is. Research also shows that TV can cause problems with pregnancy – premature birth or low birth weight. It can also be passed to a baby during the birth and cause an infection in the baby's vagina. This doesn't happen often, but when it does it's very serious.

How is TV passed on?
Through unprotected sex.

How to recognise TV
Up to half of all infected people don't have symptoms. If they do, the following signs may appear up to twenty one days after infection.

Girls: a vaginal discharge that's thin and frothy with a musty or fishy smell; a sore, itchy vagina; a sore lower tummy; pain when weeing or having sex.

Boys don't usually have any symptoms. If they do, they may have a white discharge from their penis and pain when peeing.

Tests and treatment for TV
A doctor or nurse will take a swab from affected areas and may ask for a urine sample. Treatment is with antibiotics, so don't drink alcohol until you've finished the course. TV won't go away on its own. If you're pregnant, you should tell the doctor or nurse so that they can discuss with you whether it will be helpful to have any treatment.

Protecting against TV
Use condoms every time you have sex.

Now you know all about how to protect yourself from STIs and from unwanted pregancies. But will you do it?

Developing Your Sense of
Self-Presevation

The chances are that you already knew a lot about STIs, and contraceptive protection, if not all of it. You might even feel thoroughly fed up with having endless warnings and scary information shoved down your throat. But here's a weird fact: it's not just ignorant people who put themselves at risk. You'd be amazed at how many smart, savvy, clued-up teenagers understand all the dangers . . . and still go right ahead and have sex without protecting themselves against unwanted pregnancy or disease.

What we all need to develop is a *sense of self-preservation.* When you have an in-built sense of self-preservation, you feel scared stiff at the slightest hint of danger. You feel a strong urge to protect yourself at all costs. You're not bothered by the prospect of missing out on some fun if the alternative is putting your life on the line. And instead of having a feeling, deep-down, that nothing bad is going to happen to you, you have a sneaking suspicion that if anything bad *can* happen, it probably will. This way of thinking often comes with age – although some people never develop it at all. What's for sure, though, is that lots of people start having sex *long* before they start thinking this way. That's why so many people take risks.

So where does all this leave you? You can know everything there is to know and agree that it all makes perfect sense. Then the big moment comes and somehow it all seems strangely irrelevant and totally slips from your mind. There's no doubt about it, taking care of yourself is hard work when it doesn't come naturally to you.

Try and turn safe sex into a habit – like brushing your teeth. If you force yourself to think about protection enough times, it should begin to come more naturally. Worry more. If scary thoughts about pregnancy and AIDS pop into your head, don't push them away and try to think about something else – dwell on them. Use your imagination. Scare yourself. It could save your life.

Part 3
GETTING DOWN
TO BUSINESS

So. By now you should be very knowledgeable indeed. You've explored your own body and that of the opposite sex; you've examined your attitudes and worked hard at your sexual awareness; you're all clued up about safe sex . . . Now it's about time to look at what this sex business is all about!

Chapter 7

Sex:
Everything You Ever
Wanted To Know

This chapter is all about the physical side of things: exactly what goes on behind closed doors, or – as the case may be – in cars, behind the bike sheds and anywhere else people get down to their personal business.

Hopefully, this chapter will help you know more about what to expect from sex. But don't forget that however well informed you are, sex is all about learning as you go. After all, you could read a hundred books about riding a bicycle, but it wouldn't really teach you how to get your balance – you wouldn't find out about that until you were actually on the seat!

This chapter won't turn you into some kind of sex expert, but it's still handy. Why? Because the better informed you are, the less nervous you'll be, and the less nervous you are, the more you'll enjoy the whole experience.

You'll find information on:

- Snogging
- Getting Off With Someone
- Oral Sex
- Sexual Intercourse

Here are the answers to all the questions you could want to ask . . .

Snogging

I've never snogged anyone. How do you do it?
A fair definition of a *snog* or a *French kiss* would be a kiss between two people who have their mouths open. Technically speaking, a proper French kiss would also involve tongues, and go on for longer than two seconds. It doesn't sound too difficult in principal, but people tend to get very, very nervous about not doing it right, especially if they've never done it before, or if they've only ever had snogs they didn't enjoy. The good news is that once you've got the hang of the basics, which shouldn't be too difficult, there's no 'right' way to snog, so you don't need to worry about doing it wrong. There are a few things to avoid, though. Here are the guidelines:

• No matter how you kiss, you'll get many, many extra points just for having a mouth that smells and tastes nice and lips that feel soft. Brushing your teeth and using lip balm regularly is the key. It also helps to avoid smoking or eating things like cheese and onion crisps or garlic before a snog.

• Part your lips. Relax them totally and all the muscles around your mouth, too. Your mouth should be open just a little bit at first.

• Gently press your lips against your partner's. Don't get hung up worrying about your angle of approach: most faces fit together surprisingly well and noses and other bits rarely get in the way. If you're still nervous about this, you might want to try taking your kissing-partner's face gently in your hands so that you can keep it still while you approach, or help guide it towards you.

• If one or both of you wears glasses or a dental brace,

you might want to take this stage a bit more slowly and carefully to avoid unsexy clashing accidents!

• Never approach someone too forcefully – a head-butt is a bit of a turn-off. Don't jump in with your mouth wide open like you were going to the dentist, either. It looks unattractive, off-putting and downright scary!

• Once your lips have met, you can get down to business. This should involve a combination of a kissing motion, and tongue-contact.

• The kissing motion ideally involves brushing your lips together, squashing them together firmly, and opening and closing your mouth slightly like you're tasting the other person's lips. It shouldn't involve mashing your lips so hard against the other person's that they can't breathe, and nor should your mouth ever end up too far open (it's not a competition to see how much of their mouth you can fit in yours).

• Tongue contact should be tentative at first, then just about anything goes. Just be sure to keep your tongue soft and bendy, not hard and pointy. Also, avoid excessive slobbering, swirling it round and round like a washing machine, or shoving it so far into your partner's mouth that they feel sick or suffocated.

• Relax, enjoy it, and do whatever comes naturally. If you feel like closing your eyes, feel free; if you don't, don't.

• Don't worry about skill – always remember that if someone fancies you, they'll enjoy kissing you no matter how you're doing it.

• Once you feel confident, be inventive! Delicately biting your partner's lip can be very sexy. Alternating between snogging and kissing your partner's neck is usually a popular move. Use your imagination and do whatever feels nice.

• Always pay close attention to how someone is reacting.

If you're not sure that your partner is enjoying the kiss or some aspect of it (too much tongue, maybe?), lighten up a bit and see what they do. If they are definitely trying to close their mouth or finish the kiss, back off right away!

• If you've never kissed anyone before, and you're very nervous, it can help to have a little practise on the back of your hand!

Getting Off With Someone

What's actually involved in 'getting off with' someone?
This is a term which describes the large selection of activities that can go on during a passionate snogging session. An old-fashioned phrase for this is *heavy petting*, and some people also refer to it as *touching up*. In America (and therefore probably in most of the films you've seen) it's called *making out*. All these terms can refer to something that's fairly innocent, and also to something far more heavy. They cover just about anything from general cuddling and rubbing up and down against each other, to fondling and groping someone's breasts, bum or crotch through their clothes, to steamy touchings underneath clothes, or with the clothes undone or removed. It can also mean much more intimate stuff, like kissing, licking or sucking someone's nipples, putting fingers inside a girl's vagina, touching her clitoris and touching a boy's penis. It can even mean masturbating your partner, ie, playing with their penis or clitoris in a way that's designed to make them have an orgasm. Phew!

Many teenagers find that for a while they enjoy getting off with each other even more than sex, because they feel more relaxed with the idea. It all seems less of a big deal – there's no pressure and you don't have to worry so much about protection. It's also exciting and passionate – all in all, a very nice experience indeed, and one which proves that you don't have to have full-on, penetrative sex to have fun.

So can you have an orgasm without having actual sex?
Oh yes. In fact, a girl is more likely to come this way than during sex, as her clitoris is likely to get the kind of attention that causes orgasms. For both partners, all that rubbing, groping and general excitement is often a strong enough combination to make them come. If you're masturbating each other, it's even more likely.

Do a lot of people do that?
Sure, if they feel comfortable enough together. Masturbating a boy is commonly called a *hand-job*, or *wanking* or *wanking off*, just like regular masturbation. There's no particular word for masturbating a girl, but some people call it *touching up* or the ever-popular *wanking off* again.

How do you do it?
Generally speaking, the idea is to touch and move your partner's sensitive bits exactly the same way they would if they were playing with themselves. Unfortunately, you're unlikely to have the faintest clue of how that's done! Check back to Chapter 2 to remind yourself of the basics. Here are some more pointers:

How to make a boy feel wonderful (and hopefully have an orgasm)
  • Firmly grip the penis just below the 'head' (see page 5 for a diagram), then start rhythmically moving your hand up and down the shaft, right from the base to the top. If you're gripping firmly enough, you should find that your hand slides easily up and down without ever losing contact.

• If the boy looks like he's happy with this, you can start moving your hand faster, and make the up and down movement a bit shorter, concentrating on moving over just the top half of the penis, especially the bit where the shaft meets the head, which feels especially nice.

• It's important to try and maintain the same speed and rhythm throughout, and keep your grip firm – not too tight, but not too delicate either.

• If your partner moves your hand into a new position, or says 'Faster!', don't feel insulted – he's not criticising you, just making things easier for you by letting you know what he likes.

• Lots of boys really like having their balls (testicles) 'cupped' or stroked while all this is going on – but be gentle – they're very delicate and sensitive!

• You'll know for sure when the boy has come, because semen will spurt out of the top of his penis and he'll probably make some kind of noise or exclamation! Don't stop the movement or take your hand away until the spurting is finished.

• Some boys come very quickly (it could be as quick as a few seconds, especially if he was very excited to start with), others take longer.

• It's polite to avoid going 'Eeeeew! Yuk!' and staring in disgust at your hands, clothes, or anything else that the spunk has ended up on!

• If you've been at it for ages and ages without your partner coming, and your arm feels like it's going to drop off, it's best to rest for a bit. If you really want to give up, do. You could even suggest that he finishes off the job for you – this means he ends up happy, and you get the golden opportunity to see an expert at work and learn from it – after all boys know their penises better than anyone else!

• There are other methods of making a boy feel nice or

have an orgasm. Many boys like to put their penis under their partner's armpit and move it in and out – it sounds funny, but it works! Also, if a girl has largish breasts, she can hold them together to form a snug place for a willy to slide in and out between. This is most easily done if the boy is sitting on top of the girl, so if the boy is loads heavier than the girl, it's best avoided!

How to make a girl feel wonderful (and hopefully have an orgasm)

• Many boys think that girls masturbate by sticking penis-shaped objects in themselves, and therefore to play with a girl, you have to use your finger like a penis. If you read Chapter 2, you'll know this isn't the case. Having said that, some girls do thoroughly enjoy their partner sliding their fingers quickly in and out of her, like a penis (this is sometimes rather crudely called *finger-fucking),* but most girls are unlikely to actually have an orgasm like that.

• A girl feels most sexual pleasure in her clitoris, so that's the bit to concentrate on. Whereas the penis isn't hard to find (unless you're really short-sighted), the girl's clitoris is a slightly trickier customer. Taking a good look at the diagram in Chapter 1 should help, but if you're in the height of passion, you're not going to want to say, 'Hang on a sec whilst I have a really close look at your privates'.

You'll actually need to find it by touch. Here's how: gently put your hand between your partner's legs and try to find the warm, damp area where the lips of her vagina meet. Lightly push one of your fingers in a tiny bit (you're not trying to get inside her vagina, just between the lips) and slide it slowly upwards until you feel that the gap has stopped. Here, or a tiny bit higher up, you should feel a tiny bobble. This is it!

• When you touch the clitoris, make sure you're touching the little bit of skin that covers it, or the whole area around it, not the actual clitoris (which is very sensitive). Try doing it with one or two fingers, pressing it with very light pressure, making tiny movements either up and down, or round and round, keeping up a steady rhythm. You could also stroke or rub the whole area with the palm of your hand or your fingers. Never be too rough.

• If you've got the right place and movement, your partner should be enjoying it lots. If not, she might helpfully replace your hand in a slightly different spot. Don't feel insulted – she's just helping you get to know her better!

• If your fingers are a bit damp, it can help make your movements smoother. You can use the girl's natural lubrication, or just lick your fingers.

• It's essential to understand that girls' orgasms are different to guys'. A boy would probably come from being wanked off even if he was in a very unsexy situation, because it's largely a physical reaction. A girl, however, might not be able to come even if she wanted to, for a number of reasons, including being embarrassed, nervous, pressured or distracted.

• Because girls usually don't spurt anything out when they have an orgasm, and because they don't always thrash around and shriek like women do in movies, it could be hard to tell when your partner has come. If you're lucky, she might make a noise or gasp, or she might shudder or go tense for a brief moment. She may also move your hand away, because once a girl has come, her clitoris usually feels too sensitive to be touched for a while. If you're still in doubt, ask!

• If you've been at it for ages, and it doesn't seem like your partner is going to come, don't feel too bad. Remember that you can enjoy getting off with each other (and sex) without having an orgasm.

• Interestingly enough, some girls can also come from having other parts of their bodies touched in the right way. A girl with super-sensitive breasts can have an orgasm without her partner even touching her clitoris, if he or she strokes, caresses, licks or sucks her boobs. It's also not unheard of for girls to be able to come from having their backs or tummies stroked or their hair touched and played with!

• Unlike boys, girls can come many times in one session. Although the clitoris feels sensitive right after an orgasm, it usually feels fine again quite soon, and you'll find that if you carry on playing with your partner, she'll be able to come again, if you both want to try.

• The official record for the most orgasms in one session is fifty! It's held by an American woman who was helping sex-researchers with a study of women's orgasms at the time. She claimed afterwards that she thought she could have managed a few more! This is obviously rather extreme, but it just goes to illustrate how different girls are to boys in this way – whilst the average guy can only manage about four orgasms in one sex session (and it's likely to be less), the average girl can just keep on going!

The above descriptions may sound a bit clinical and yukky. That's because they don't mention all the little things that make playing with each other like this loving and passionate instead of technical. Kissing, saying nice things, stroking your partner's hair or body, cuddling, pressing your body up against theirs, and showing or telling them how much you're enjoying yourself is what makes the difference.

Does it matter if a boy doesn't come when you're wanking him? Someone told me that it was dangerous for them . . .
You might have heard about something that boys can get, sometimes called *blue balls*. When a boy gets very sexually excited, blood rushes into his penis (giving him an erection) and also his testicles, making them feel firmer and fuller,

right? When he has an orgasm, all that blood rushes away again. If he doesn't have one, the blood goes away and everything goes back to normal eventually, but it takes much longer. Until that happens, a boy can sometimes have an uncomfortable, tight, achy feeling in his balls, and they can also look slightly blue (because of all those full blood vessels).

This can be a bit scary, and a bit annoying, but it's not at all dangerous. Some boys try to use blue balls as an excuse to put pressure on their girlfriends to have sex, saying that if they don't do it, they'll be in terrible pain or suffer terrible damage. This just isn't true, so boys: don't say it, and girls: don't believe a word of it!

Can girls get blue balls too?
Obviously girls don't have balls, but yes, experts have discovered that there is a similar thing that girls can get if they get very, very aroused without coming. Again, it's a swollen, achy feeling in the privates (and sometimes a mild, low tummy-ache), but although it's annoying, it can't do you any damage.

Is foreplay the same as getting off with each other?
Pretty much. The difference is that foreplay means you're leading up to having full, penetrative sex, while getting off with each other is done just for the fun of it, without leading up to anything else. The other difference is that in foreplay, you'd probably want to avoid the boy coming, in case he didn't manage to get hard again for sex.

Do you have to have foreplay before you have sex?
No, but it helps to get you both relaxed and in the mood, so it's a nice idea. Foreplay is especially useful for girls, because it can get them excited enough to make the natural wetness which makes sex more comfortable.

Can you get pregnant from just getting off with someone, or from foreplay?

It depends. You only need a tiny bit of semen to find its way into a girl's vagina for her to get pregnant, and it *is* possible for this to happen accidentally during masturbating or foreplay. If either of you get semen on your hands, it could also end up just where you don't want it. It's safe to say that if a girl's got her knickers on, she's pretty unlikely to get pregnant, but remember that knickers are not considered a reliable form of contraception! To be safe, always be fully aware of where semen goes. And wear a condom if things get *really* steamy – even if you don't have full-on sex.

What about catching diseases?

Boys aren't really at risk from masturbating or foreplay. Girls have a bigger risk if there's semen about. If you've both got your undies on, or the boy doesn't come at all, we're talking about pretty safe sex. However, if you introduce oral sex to the mix, you've got all the risks that come with it. Many STIs can be passed on through oral sex – see Chapter 6. When you have oral sex you must always protect yourselves by using a condom for boys and a dental dam for girls. (Dental dams are latex squares available from sexual health clinics.)

Oral Sex

What's oral sex?

Oral means 'to do with the mouth' and oral sex is the general term for doing things to your partner's privates with your mouth. When you have oral sex with a boy, it's technically called *fellatio*, but you're more likely to have heard it called a *blow job, giving head, sucking off* or *going down* on someone.

The proper word for oral sex with a girl is *cunnilingus,* but again, few people actually use it – most people talk about *going down* on someone or use terms like *muff-diving* and *eating pussy.*

Oral sex is a normal, natural, nice part of sex. Still, a lot of people of both sexes don't like doing it to other people, and quite a few girls and some boys (but not many!) don't particularly enjoy having it done to them. This can be because they don't like the way it feels, and sometimes it's because they feel self-conscious about someone's head being that close to their privates – the worry and embarrassment that their bits might look or smell funny stops them from being able to relax and enjoy it.

As with any other activity, you should always be thoughtful about what your partner does and doesn't want to do.

Can you get pregnant by having oral sex?

As long as no semen goes near her vagina, a girl can't get pregnant by having or giving oral sex. However, there is a risk of catching an STI (see *What about catching diseases* opposite), so you need to use a condom or a dental dam to be safe when giving or receiving oral sex.

How do you do it?

The general idea of oral sex is to lick, kiss and suck your partner's sensitive bits. This usually feels very nice for the person on the receiving end. For the person doing the work, it can be quite tiring, and it must be said that most of the pleasure comes from knowing your partner is enjoying it.

If you still feel you'd like some more specific info about it, read on:

Giving a Boy a Blow Job

The first thing to do when you're giving a boy a blow job is to put a condom on his penis. See page 87 for details of how.

The second thing to know about a blow job is not to blow! Blowing on the penis as if it was hot soup won't do anything at all. Yes, the name is misleading. Stupid, isn't it?

With your partner's help, you will soon find your own special ways to please him with oral sex, but here are a few tips that might help to kick things off:

• Open your mouth and lower your head onto your partner's penis, guiding it with your hands until it's a couple of centimetres or so inside your mouth. If you feel like you're choking, gagging or retching, it's probably in too far!

• Close your mouth around the tip of the penis, being sure to protect it from your teeth either by keeping them well parted, or curling your lips over them. Start sucking to create a vacuum pressure inside your mouth. You can get an idea of what that feels like by sucking your thumb hard with your mouth closed.

• Grip the base of the penis and move your head up and down, still sucking all the time, so that the penis is slipping in and out between your lips.

• When you've got a comfortable rhythm going, you could try flicking your tongue around the tip of the penis at the same time.

• Some people also move their penis-gripping hand up and down in time with their mouth.

• Some people also like to stop occasionally to lick the tip of the penis and the bit where the head meets the shaft (see diagram on page 5) with fast, flicking tongue movements, or lick up and down the whole length of the penis, before taking it in their mouth again and carrying on.

• Many boys like to have their testicles licked, kissed and gently sucked too (but never forget how delicate and sensitive they are).

• As soon as possible after he's come and whilst his penis is still hard, remove the condom as described on page 87. Remember to tie a knot at the open end of it to contain the semen, wrap it and throw it away – don't flush it down the loo!

Going Down on a Girl

The first thing to do when you're giving oral sex to a girl is to practise safe sex by placing a dental dam over the area of her clitoris and vagina. Dental dams are pieces of latex rubber, about 10cm square, which are available from sexual health clinics. Like male condoms, they allow you to give oral sex to a girl without your saliva coming into contact with her vaginal fluids, or vice versa. Once it's in place . . .

Remember the clitoris? That's your main target again, only this time you're using your mouth and tongue instead of your hands. You and your partner will discover what works best for you, but here are some tips to get you started . . .

• There are a few different techniques. For instance you can make repeated, rhythmic kissing and sucking motions, you can lick slowly and you can flick your tongue in quick, sharp, lapping motions. You can also suck and flick your tongue at the same time. Why not try everything, and see what your partner likes best?

• Always mind your teeth!

• If your partner seems uncomfy and jumpy, you might be touching her clitoris too directly, which feels very sensitive – try to avoid doing that by working around it instead. The dental dam should help shield it too.

• You don't have to just concentrate on the clitoris – licking and kissing all around that area feels nice too.

• Lots of girls find that oral sex makes them have an orgasm quite quickly. Others find it takes longer, and many more rarely come during oral sex at all. The best thing to do, until you know what the score is with your partner, is to carry on for as long as she's enjoying it and you're not getting too knackered! If she doesn't seem to be enjoying it, or she seems to be getting tired of it, move on to doing something else.

Sexual Intercourse

So what about the real thing?
Call it what you will – *sexual intercourse, penetration, copulation, coitus, love-making, shagging, fucking, screwing, humping, shafting, poking, rumping, rodgering, going all-the-way* – penetrative sex is seen as the big deal to end all big deals in the world of sexual encounters. This is quite strange, considering that oral sex, playing with one another and even general petting are pretty intense, intimate experiences, too. If you've done any of those things, then you've experienced quite a lot of what sex is about, and may not find penetration to be the huge leap into the unknown that you'd expected.

Right. Let's say that me and my partner know each other, like each other and trust each other enough to want to take things further. We've talked about contraception and safe sex and have a condom ready. We're both relaxed and happy, we've just had a snog or foreplay or whatever, and now we're ready to go all the way! What happens next?
Just as no two people are totally identical, no two love-making sessions are ever the same either! Just how you and your partner will enjoy making love is up to the two of you, but here are a few basic things you can expect.

• At some point you'll remove some or all of your clothes – your pants at the very least, or it might be a bit tricky!

• When the boy's penis is hard, you'll put on a condom.

152

• Once you're both in a comfortable position, it's time for the boy to slip his penis into the girl. The boy can take charge of this bit, but it's *tonnes* easier if you do it together. The girl can help by either guiding the penis with her hand, or just wriggling herself into the right position.

• Once the penis is comfortably inside, the boy moves his hips so that it thrusts in and out. The boy will probably set the pace, because he's moving his penis in a way that excites him. It is possible for a couple to have sex without the girl budging an inch, but it's extremely boring for the girl, and quite boring for the boy too. The girl can move too, in time with her partner, although these movements don't always come as easily and naturally to girls as they do to boys.

• Most girls like the feeling of having a boy's penis inside them, but they don't always get that much in the way of amazing physical sensations from what's going on inside. For many girls, the nice feelings come from the whole area around the vagina – yes, we're talking about the clitoris again.

Lots of girls find that just the in-and-out motion moves all their parts in a way that feels nice, but others find they need to actually press their clitoris against the boy to get that exciting feeling. Some girls solve this problem by touching their clitorises, or having their partner do it for them, while they're making love. This is easier in some positions than others (see further down).

• It's pretty rare for a boy not to come during sex, as long as he is relaxed and happy. However, it's remarkably common for a girl not to, especially if she hasn't had sex many times, because she's not yet familiar with what she needs to do. Most girls eventually find a particular position, movement or other trick that makes the difference. The good news is that the older a woman gets, the more likely she is to be able to come during sex. But remember: as wonderful as orgasms can be, they're really not the be-all and end-all: you *can* enjoy sex without having one.

153

What's the best position to have sex in?
There are lots of different positions you can have sex in, and
which is the best is a matter of personal taste. Mind you, you
don't have to pick just one – you can change over as many
times as you like! These are the best known, most popular
positions:

• *Boy on top* – the girl lies down, or sits and leans back,
with her legs apart.
Advantages: You can kiss, and see each other's faces. The
boy can move freely.
Disadvantages: The girl can't move that freely.

• *Girl on top* – the boy lies down, but with his knees a bit
bent so that he can still move his hips freely. His partner either
lies or half-sits on top, with her knees on either side of him.
Advantages: You can kiss, and see each other's faces. The
girl can move freely, and is more likely to have an orgasm,
because she can control the movements. If the girl sits up, her
partner can touch her breasts and clitoris.
Disadvantages: The boy can't move that freely. Some girls
feel shy about being 'in charge'.

• *From behind* – this position is sometimes called *doggie-
style*. The girl kneels on all fours with her partner behind her.
You can also do it so that the girl is lying on her front with her
partner on top of her.
Advantages: Both partners can move freely. The boy can
touch the girl's breasts and clitoris. His penis fits more snugly
in this position. Boys who like looking at their partner's bum
get a nice treat!
Disadvantages: You can't kiss or see each other's faces. If the
boy has a very long penis, it might go in too deep in this
position and be uncomfortable for the girl.

• *Side by side* – the boy and girl lie on their sides, either
facing each other, or with the boy behind the girl, which is
sometimes called *spooning*.

Advantages: Both partners can move freely. You both have at least one arm free to cuddle and touch each other. You can kiss and see each other (if you're doing it face to face). Not too tiring for either partner.

Disadvantages: Can be tricky to get the penis in at first.

• *Sitting down* – this is usually done with the girl sitting on the boy's lap.

Advantages: You can kiss and see each other's faces. Both of you have your arms free, so you can cuddle and touch each other too.

Disadvantages: Can be tiring for the boy, and he can't move his hips that freely.

• *Standing up* – unless you've got great balance, you need a wall as support for this position!

Advantages: You can kiss and see each other's faces. Both of you have your arms free for touching and cuddling. You can use this position in exciting places like showers and cupboards!

Disadvantages: Can be tiring for both partners and dead tricky (or impossible) if there's a big height difference.

• There are other positions, but most of them are just variations on these basic ones. For instance, boy on top, but with the girls' legs in the air, so her knees are by her head and her feet are resting on her partner's shoulders.

Other alternative positions can be dictated by where you are. For instance, in the kitchen, the girl might sit on a low counter and wrap her legs round her partner as he stands facing her. In the living room she can perch on the edge of the sofa with her legs open, while he kneels in front of her. There's probably a position for every room in the house if you have the energy and imagination for it!

What's anal sex?

Anal is a word that means 'to do with your bum', and anal sex is when a boy puts his penis into someone's anus (bum hole).

It's also sometimes known as *buggery*, or *buggering* someone. The anus has lots of nerve endings, so some people enjoy anal sex, but it can also be quite painful. It's the riskiest form of sex from the STI point of view – because the inside of the back passage is tight and the skin tears easily, allowing for the exchange of both partner's secretions. For this reason you must always wear a condom if you have anal sex – and an extra-strong one is recommended.

Do boys who are gay always have anal sex?
No. Two boys together will usually do the same things that a boy and a girl do together – kissing, cuddling, touching, playing with each other and having oral sex. Sometimes – but not always – they also decide to have anal sex. Like everyone else, they have their own, individual tastes and preferences.

How do two girls have sex?
Many people imagine that lesbian sex involves one girl pretending to be a man, and even perhaps wearing a pretend penis, or *dildo*. This isn't usually the case, and although some gay girls *do* enjoy penetrative sex – using their fingers or sex toys – many don't. Girls who are gay want to have sex with other girls because they like girls, and girls' bodies – therefore they're usually not very bothered that there's no penis involved. Like gay men, lesbians usually do the same things that heterosexuals do – kissing, cuddling, touching, playing with each other and having oral sex.

How do you have sex if you've got a physical disability?
It goes without saying that people with disabilities enjoy sex as much as anyone else, and that all the information and advice in this book applies to them equally. Young people with disabilities need to be able to talk to their partners about how their disabilities might affect what they do together. There are

many, many ways to express sexual feelings, and if certain positions and forms of love-making are difficult or impossible, then the two of them can explore to find ways that are comfortable to both. It goes without saying again that sex doesn't just mean sexual intercourse or having an orgasm – cuddling, touching and kissing your partner can be just as satisfying and pleasurable for both.

On the practical side, some people's individual disabilities and the medication they might be taking may have an effect on what kind of contraception they can use. It's very important to let the doctor or nurse know exactly what your disabilities are and what medication you're on when you're choosing the right contraception for you.

There's a helpful publication that you can download from www.cafamily.org.uk called *Growing Up, Sex and Relationships: A Booklet for Young Disabled People*

People in films always make lots of noise during sex. Do you have to do that?
People in films seem to think you have to, but you don't really! Just do whatever comes naturally. Some people don't feel the urge to make much noise at all, others find they make all sorts of sounds without even realising it – everything from gentle panting (because they're breathless from moving around a lot or just sheer excitement) to gasps, grunts, groans, moans and even shrieks and yells (usually because they're enjoying themselves so much). Generally, though, people don't make half as much noise in real life as they do in films!

Is it OK to talk during sex?
Again, being natural is always the best thing. If you feel like saying something, say it (as long as it's to do with sex or how you feel about your partner – suddenly announcing that you don't fancy Arsenal's chances in the Championship probably

won't go down too well). Appreciative comments are always nice, because they make your partner feel confident and good. They can also help let your partner know what you like (for instance – 'I love it when you do that').

Whatever you say, make sure you mean it, and avoid comments you've heard in films or books, especially if you don't feel 100% comfortable saying them. Things like 'Oooh baby, that feels good', 'Give it to me, big boy' or 'I'm gonna make you purr like a kitten' normally sound fairly stupid!

What's talking dirty?

This is when you pay a compliment, talk about what you're doing or reveal something else you'd like to do, using more rude words than normal. Lots of people find talking dirty an incredible turn-on, whether they're talking or listening. Others find it scary, threatening or off-putting, so if you're planning to try, start gently and check your partner's reaction before going any further.

What happens if I accidentally do something embarrassing during sex? I think I'd die!

Most people can tell you at least one embarrassing thing that's happened to them during sex, from farting or burping to getting hiccups or a fit of the giggles. It's reassuring to know that these things happen to everybody – although you'd never know it from watching movies and TV, would you?

Sex in real life is not all unbridled passions and soft lighting. It's also messy, funny and sometimes a bit silly. Even if you can fight the occasional natural urge to fart or burp, your body can make all sorts of weird noises during sex. Tummies can rumble, two chests pressing together can make air escape in a very farty way, and billions of girls are horrified to find out the hard way about *fanny-farts* – a highly embarrassing parping noise that can occur when air escapes from the vagina when the boy takes his penis out after sex!

The point is that none of these things are a big deal unless you turn them into one. If something embarrassing happens to you, just go 'Oops!' or ignore it altogether, then try to get back in the right mood by reassuring yourself that it wasn't so terrible. After all, if you and your partner are close enough to have sex, you should be comfortable enough to cope with a silly little thing like this. If your partner is mature and nice, they'll either laugh along with you or ignore it, and not mention it afterwards. If they're stupid about it, or tell other people, ditch them pronto and be thankful that you discovered how immature and mean they were before you got any further into a relationship with them.

Can I have sex during my period?
If you and your partner don't mind, there's no reason not to. Lots of people feel fine about it, others don't. The only way to find out how your partner feels is to ask. If you do have sex during your period, it's smart to put down a towel first, to avoid staining the bed (sofa, floor, car seat, whatever).

What do you think about during sex?
If you're thoroughly enjoying the sex, then you'll be drifting away, thinking about nothing in particular. If it's your first time, or your first time with a new partner, you might be thinking more specifically about what you're doing.

Some people deliberately think about sexy things, or fantasise, which can add enormously to the pleasure of sex. Many – especially girls, find that fantasising can make it much easier to have an orgasm.

Is it wrong to imagine that the person you're having sex with is somebody else?
Who's to say what's right or wrong? Many, many people enjoy

159

shutting their eyes and pretending that they're actually shagging David Beckham or Cheryl Cole or whoever, whether it's a fleeting thought, or a long, elaborate fantasy. It's pretty harmless to do this now and again, as long as you don't tell your partner about it. If you do it every time you have sex, and you don't think you could possibly get excited without doing it, then perhaps you should think carefully about your true feelings for your partner, and ask yourself if you really want to be having sex with them at all.

How long does it take to have sex?

You've probably noticed by now that there's no such thing as normal, where sex is concerned. Sometimes it can last for an hour or more. Other times it's over in a few minutes. If the boy suffers from *premature ejaculation* (coming too quickly), it could even be a matter of seconds – see page 185 for more details. Between ten minutes and half an hour – including foreplay – is about average. People often brag – or write song lyrics – about having sex 'all night long', but longer is not necessarily better. If you really did it all night long the chances are that you'd both end up knackered, achy, sore and a bit bored.

Don't bother worrying about how long sex goes on for; it's not a competition. The most important thing is that you both enjoy it.

How do you know when it's over?

In theory, sex is over when both partners have come. In reality, it's over when the boy has come, because, with all the best will in the world, he's not going to be able to carry on shagging after that. Obviously this could put a bit of pressure on the boy to make sure that his partner comes first, or at the same time. This is easier said than done, since it's difficult, if not impossible, to stop yourself from coming if you're close to it –

especially when you're young. Another fact to consider is that the girl may not manage to come at all, especially if it's her first time. If both partners still felt in a sexy mood once the boy has come, they could start cuddling and kissing again, and the boy could try to give his partner an orgasm by playing with her. There's also nothing to say that you have to have sex just once in an evening – if no one's tired, and the boy can manage to get hard, you can do it all again!

What do you do after you've finished having sex?
As soon as he's come, the boy needs to withdraw his penis and remove the condom before he goes soft, then dispose of it properly. Once that's out of the way, it all depends on how you feel. Some people like to lie cuddling for a while. Others prefer to roll apart and get their breath back. There's no sense in rushing about frantically when you could be enjoying what's sometimes called the *afterglow* – the delicious warm, happy, loving and close feeling that comes from having good sex with someone you really care about.

Chapter 8

Great Sex

Now you know more than a bit about the basics, here are some tips and suggestions to make good sex even more enjoyable!

In this chapter you'll find:

- Great Expectations . . .
- So What Makes Sex Great?
- Do You Have to Be in Love to Have Great Sex?
- Making Great Sex Even Better!
- *More* Secrets of Great Sex

Great Expectations

Or should that be Great *Sex*pectations?!

Here are two typical comments from people about their first sexual experiences:

'I thought that losing my virginity would be the most amazing thing that ever happened to me, but afterwards, all I could think was 'Is that it? That can't be what all the fuss is about!' I didn't really enjoy it much at all. Is there something wrong with me?'

'I recently had sex for the first time and it was quite nice, but also a bit disappointing because it wasn't at all how I expected it to be . . .'

No matter how much you know about sex, how well prepared you are and how lovely your partner is, you can never guarantee that sex is going to turn out perfectly. Most people find that at best, their first sexual experience isn't quite the way they thought it would be, and at worst, can't figure out for the life of them why anyone actually bothers doing it at all!

Sometimes – but not all that often – people find that magic comes together the very first time they do it. Others feel a bit disappointed, as they imagined that 'the earth was going to move', that there'd be fireworks and that their whole lives would change for the better.

Think about it this way: two people are going skiing for the first time. One is expecting to have a wonderful adventure, skiing down a nice, gentle little slope and gradually getting confident on their skis. The other has spent ages day-dreaming about swooping through the air off towering ski-jumps at seventy miles an hour. When they finally go skiing, they both have a pretty good time, but one of them is going to be happy about it and the other is probably going to feel disappointed.

You see, it's not about what actually happens, but how it compares to what you expected. Sex is the same deal, and there's only one way to make sure sex lives up to all your expectations: have very realistic expectations.

Sex is rarely anything like it is in the movies. That's not to say that it's not as exciting or romantic or fabulous. It's just that everyone does it differently, and you'll enjoy sex much more if you don't have any set ideas about how it 'should' be.

Sex is not about doing things in any particular order or style. It's about enjoying yourself and making sure that your partner is enjoying it too.

So What Makes Sex Great?

There's no magic formula for great sex – it's more complex than that. However, there's a good chance that sex will be wonderful if:

- You and your partner are relaxed and happy.
- Both of you really want to have sex and have no doubts about it.
- You've talked about sex and listened to how the other feels.
- You both fancy each other like mad.
- You're protecting yourselves against pregnancy and diseases.
- You both feel fairly comfy with your own bodies.
- Neither of you feels embarrassed or guilty about having sex or enjoying it.
- Neither of you feels any pressure to be 'good' in bed, or 'live up to' your partner's expectations.
- You really want your partner to enjoy the experience as much as you do.
- You both feel comfortable enough to laugh or shrug it off

if anything goes wrong, or if anything embarrassing happens.

• You know you'll still care about each other even if the sex doesn't turn out to be that brilliant.

You might notice that most of these factors depend on your having a good relationship. This is no coincidence – the best sex happens between people who care about each other and feel comfortable together.

Do You Have to Be in Love to Have Great Sex ?

If you're actually in love, the chances of having great sex are much better than if you're not. It's true, though, that some people manage to have great sex without having a relationship at all. Usually, they just adore the experience of sex, the way that other people adore surfing or horse-riding, and they're not that bothered about the emotional side. Sex for sex's sake *can* be wonderful – if the two people involved think the same way. However, it can be hard for someone who wants to shag just for fun, no strings attached, to find a like-minded partner. Most people want some kind of relationship, and have sex for deeper, more emotional reasons.

Making Great Sex Even Better!

Once you've got the right person and the right circumstances you're well on the road to great sex. The longer you and your partner stay together, the better the sex will get. There's no mystery to this – it's because the better you get to know each other, the more you'll both know what the other likes.

There are two kinds of pleasure you can feel during sex. One is basic physical pleasure. The other is the satisfaction and pride of knowing that your partner is enjoying the whole thing as much as you are.

Here's what you need to discover to get that perfect balance:

Find out what your partner likes

First, look for clues. Is your partner having a good time? Are there some times during sex when they seem happier than others? Do they enjoy lots of foreplay before sex or do they just want to get on with it? Do they seem keen to cuddle and kiss during sex? Do they prefer a particular position? Do they want to try lots of different positions or just stick with one? Apart from simply observing and guessing, it's helpful to ask questions. Ask, 'Do you like it like this?' when you're making love in a certain position or in a certain way (harder, softer, faster, slower). Or you could say, 'Does this feel nice?' when you're touching, licking, nibbling, whatever. A good combination of asking and observing will help you get a really clear picture of everything your partner likes.

Find out what they don't like

This is just as important as what they *do* like, so always be alert for signs that your partner is feeling uncomfortable or would rather be doing something else. If you're trying something new for the first time (anything from ear-nibbling to talking dirty to oral sex) and you're not sure if your partner is enjoying it, always ask early on. There's nothing worse for both of you than spending ages doing something that one of you doesn't like.

Let your partner know your likes and dislikes

It's equally important that your partner gets to enjoy the same happy balance between giving and getting pleasure. Do everything you can to help. Don't be afraid to say, 'That feels great!' or 'I love it like this!' – it's flattering and encouraging as well as useful. Don't be afraid to give clues about the things you're not so keen on, either. Remember, your partner wants to please you! They will be glad to know your dislikes, not upset – especially if you tell them how much you enjoy other parts of their love-making.

More Secrets of Great Sex

There is one more very important thing to know: really great sex isn't just about boobs and bums and willies and fannies. Because these bits are the most sensitive in a sexual way, many people ignore just about everything else. This is a big mistake. There is so much other fabulous, exciting stuff you can do that doesn't involve the sexual 'target' areas, and can make your partner go completely gooey. Here are some things that you may not have thought of doing, which loads of people absolutely adore:

- Snogging during sex
- Hugging during sex
- Having their hair stroked or played with
- Having their neck nibbled, kissed, sucked, licked and nuzzled
- Having their back stroked or gently scratched
- Having their toes or fingers nibbled, kissed, sucked or licked
- Being told how gorgeous and sexy they are
- Talking about their fantasies

• Having romantic or dirty things whispered to them
. . . And there are many more. Use your imagination and let yourself go! And never forget that you're having sex with a person, not a collection of body-parts.

Chapter 9

Some Other Stuff
You Might Have Heard About

Learning about sex can be confusing. Just when you think you've got a pretty good handle on the whole affair, you hear about something from a friend, on TV, the internet or even in a pop song that sounds really, really weird. Here are some of those questions that many people would love to ask, but don't dare . . .

What's an aphrodisiac?
It's something that you eat, drink or smell, which supposedly makes you feel extra-sexy and madly keen to shag, as if by magic. You might have heard that foods like oysters, peaches and garlic are aphrodisiacs, or been told about strange things like crushed beetles (called *Spanish Fly*), or scents that are supposed to drive the opposite sex wild, like musk and perfumes containing *pheromones*. Sadly, there's no proof that any of these things work at all, so it's never worth wasting your time or money.

Is Viagra an aphrodisiac?

No. Viagra is a drug used to treat *erectile dysfunction* in men. Erectile dysfuntion means difficulty in maintaining an erection during sex. Viagra works by stimulating blood flow into the penis, which helps keep it harder for longer. It is usually prescribed to older men, and never to teenagers. Taking unprescribed Viagra as a recreational drug (ie, using it for fun) is on the increase amongst young people, and is a dangerous thing to do. It may cause serious side effects, especially if it's mixed with other drugs.

What is pornography?

Pornography – *porn* for short – consists of images, texts or films that are intended to provoke sexual excitement. Some types of pornography, such as child pornography, are illegal. Otherwise, unless a court decides that an image is 'obscene', the definition of which is that it is likely to 'deprave' or 'corrupt', almost anything goes.

With the advent of the internet it's pretty easy to access pornography, even if you're under sixteen. In fact, it can sometimes be hard to avoid it! And it provokes a lot of different opinions and feelings. Many males and a few females like to look at porn while they're masturbating, and some couples like to look at it together. Other people want to see it banned, or just feel that it's 'wrong'. Many believe that it's degrading to the people in the images and that it encourages people to see others as sex objects. Other people don't object to porn itself, but hate the way that the porn industry is run: with the models and actors usually paid a pittance and often persuaded or forced to do things they don't want to do, while the people at the top of the ladder (who are often criminals) rake in the cash.

There are still others who don't particularly like porn, but don't want to see it banned, because they believe that this would be censorship, and censorship is bad, because people should have the freedom to look at whatever they want.

As you can see, porn is a very confusing issue! At the end of the day, though, common sense should tell us:

• There's nothing wrong with looking at images of other people's bodies – as long as they are not being harmed in any way.

• You're not hurting anyone else if you look at it in private.

• You have got to be mature and intelligent enough to understand that people in real life are not necessarily going to look like, or want to do the same things you see in pornographic material.

• There's no need to worry about enjoying it, as long as it doesn't take over your life to the extent where you'd rather have a be looking at internet porn than in a loving sexual relationship.

What are vibrators?

They're things that some women use to masturbate with. A vibrator is a small, plastic, battery-operated gadget that vibrates at different speeds and is often, but not always, penis-shaped. Women hold them against their clitoris area to enjoy the sensations they give. Many women who find it difficult to have an orgasm otherwise, are able to come in this way.

Vibrators are safe, harmless and fun to use. However, because vibrators and other sex toys are likely to get covered in vaginal fluid – or semen, if it's a man's toy – you must never share them with someone else, unless you can put a condom over them.

What other kinds of sex toy are there?

A sex toy is basically any gadget designed to be used for fun during sex or masturbation. They include:

• *Dildos* – Plastic penis-shaped things that you can put inside you. Some women like these but most prefer vibrators.

• *Love eggs* – Pairs of little plastic or metal balls that you put in your vagina, where they're supposed to jiggle around and feel nice.

• *Pocket pussies* – These are artificial vaginas for men to masturbate with. They're basically hollow devices that are put over the penis, where they can be moved up and down to simulate sex. Some actually look a bit like vaginas, others come in bright colours and have knobbly bits inside for extra stimulation. They're made of soft materials like rubber, they're often lubricated and, sometimes, heated! You can also get ones that vibrate.

• *Cock rings* – Also known as penile rings, these are little tight bands of metal that men can slip down over their penis. The idea is that the penis stays harder for longer, by stopping the blood from flowing out of it. Some cock rings also have a clitoral stimulator, or a small vibrator attached to please women.

There are many, many more sex toys out there – lots of them variations on the ones mentioned above. Some people enjoy using them for masturbating alone or for spicing up sex with their partners, others are just as happy without.

What is 69?

69 is the name for a popular position for oral sex, where both partners can suck and kiss each other's bits at the same time. Basically, you lie side-by-side or one on top of the other, but head-to-tail, so that both your mouths are level with each other's crotches. It probably got its name because if you did a drawing of two pin-men in this position, it would look a bit like the number 69! It's also sometimes called *Soixante-neuf* (pronounced *swa-sont nerf*) which is the French word for the number 69.

What's a multiple orgasm? Women's magazines seem to mention them quite a lot . . .

They certainly do! A multiple orgasm means coming more than once in a very short time (like a minute or two), and it's something that only girls can experience. What happens is that, instead of coming once and that being it for a while, a girl can sometimes continue to feel excited. And if she or her partner carry on doing sexy things, it's possible for her to come again right away – and again, and again!

If this happens to you, it's lovely, but no girl should feel cheated or worried if it never happens – it's not a big deal.

What's a G-spot?

The G-spot is the name given to a particular bunch of nerve endings that can be found inside the vagina, a few centimetres up, on what's called the front wall (the side nearest to your tummy). It's named after the scientist who discovered it, Dr Ernst Grafenberg. Some women find that it's super sensitive, and say that they can have an orgasm by stimulating it with their fingers or an object, or having their partner do it with their fingers or penis (this is easiest if you're having sex 'doggie style'). Other women can't find it for the life of them, and swear that it doesn't exist – and some sex experts agree with them. Girls, if it works for you – brilliant. If not, don't worry – like multiple orgasms, finding your G-spot certainly isn't the be-all and end-all of sex!

Do boys have a G-spot?

Not exactly, but many experts say that the most similar thing is the prostate gland. This can be found inside your bum, a couple of centimetres up, on the front wall (the side nearest your tummy), and it feels like a firm lump. Some boys like to put their finger or an object up their bum to stimulate it, or enjoy their partner doing it for them. Others don't like the idea or feeling of having anything up their bum for any reason. Like the G-spot, it's no big deal – so don't worry about missing out if you can't find it, or don't want to.

Someone told me that girls fake orgasms. Why would they want to do that?

Many women fake orgasms, and they do it for all sorts of reasons – because they want to please their partner, because they're tired and they want to finish having sex, or just because it becomes a habit. Faking orgasms means that the girl's partner will assume that she is perfectly happy with her sex-life, and will carry on in the same way. If she doesn't mind not having real orgasms, it's OK, but what if she really would like to have orgasms with her partner? If he was aware of the situation, they could try out a few new things that might help her to come. But if he doesn't know that she isn't really coming, there's no way that can happen. Plus, the longer a girl goes on faking it, the more upset her partner will be if and when she eventually comes clean.

Can you tell if a girl is faking it?

Some girls are very good actresses! However, boys can look for clues if they really want to know the truth. When a girl comes, her nipples go hard and stick out more – so if your partner's nipples are still soft and flattish after she's apparently come, she might well have been pretending. Many girls also get a flush of pinkish colour over their faces, necks and chests after coming – and you definitely can't fake that! If you think your girlfriend might be faking orgasms, try to talk to her about it, if you can, without accusing her. Ask her to tell you what she enjoys you doing the most, sexually, and then you can try to work together to make sure she's as happy and satisfied as possible.

Can men fake orgasms?
Some do occasionally – for all the same reasons as women – but obviously it's much easier to get sussed out. If a boy hasn't really come, he won't ejaculate, and his girlfriend wouldn't have to be a super-detective to find out – if there's no semen, there was almost definitely no orgasm.

What is it with handcuffs? I've seen people in films and TV make out that they're something to do with sex . . .
Using handcuffs during sex is part of something called *bondage*. It's a kind of sexy game, where someone ties their partner's wrists or ankles together, or ties them to the bedposts before sex or foreplay. It's very common, and those who are into it find it dead exciting. Some people use handcuffs, others prefer rope, or something soft like a scarf or a pair of tights.

Bondage can sound terribly perverted, but there's really nothing wrong with it as long as both partners trust each other and are equally into the idea. The person who's tied up should always feel sure that their partner will quit the game right away and untie them if they change their mind at any time. If you don't know your partner well enough to be sure of that, then the game could be quite scary and threatening, and is best avoided.

Tabloids often write about 'three-in-a-bed' scandals. What's all that about?
Sex is designed for two people. However, it's not unheard of for three – two women and a man, or two men and a woman – to all go to bed together. This is called having a *threesome*. Anything can go on in a threesome, in just about any combination you can imagine, and if everyone involved is equally comfortable and happy, they can all have a lovely time. Problems often come if two of the partners are a couple,

and one gets jealous of what their other half gets up to with the third person. That's why although many people fantasise about having a threesome, not that many actually try it.

Is a threesome the same as an orgy?
No. An orgy is when four or more people get together. They were very popular in ancient Roman times, and they were debauched, excessive affairs where the wine would flow, tons of food would get eaten, and the shagging would go on for days. These days, an orgy is more likely to be called *group sex.* Group sex tends to be a sort of party where everyone takes their kit off and gets intimate with everyone else – or at least a few different people. It can happen almost anywhere – at organised or impromptu events in outdoor locations, at sex parties, nightclubs, private homes or hotel rooms.

What's S&M?
S&M stands for *Sadism and Masochism.* Sadism is when someone gets sexually turned on by hurting people, and Masochism is when someone gets sexually turned on by being hurt. S&M is the term given to what a sadist (the master) and a masochist (the victim) get up to together. It's not a particularly common sexual practice. With S&M, it's absolutely essential that both partners trust each other and set clear boundaries to prevent them from going too far and really harming each other.

My friend told me that some people enjoy spanking each other! Do they really?
Spanking can be another sex game. Some people like the idea of being playfully – or even not so playfully – smacked on the bottom during sex. Others are very much into the idea of doing it. Again, trust and setting boundaries are the keys to this game being safe and fun for both partners. Some people

only like spanking or being spanked if it doesn't really hurt, others actually like the fact that a firm smack stings a bit. If you ever decide to try spanking, be sure that you and your partner are in agreement on this subject well before you start!

When I said that I liked water-sports, my friend started giggling and said that meant that I liked people weeing on me during sex! Surely people don't do that?

People do all sorts of things, and yes, weeing on each other *is* one of them. Your friend is also right that this can be called *water-sports*. It's not particularly common, and most people probably don't much like the idea, but some people find it very exciting indeed. It's also not unheard of for people to enjoy pooing on each other, believe it or not! Obviously these practices are messy and a bit unhygienic, but if both partners are keen, why not?

I've heard people make jokes about farmers having sex with sheep. Does this really go on?

Having sex with animals is called *bestiality*. It doesn't happen a lot, but it does happen, and not just with farmers, or just with sheep. Obviously, it's unhygienic for the human and cruel and (often) dangerous for the animal. It's also illegal. However, many, many people fantasise about having their privates licked by an animal, and some even like to imagine having sex with one. Remember that fantasies are harmless, and don't mean you want them to happen in real life. Having said that, more people than you'd expect – usually teenagers – will admit to encouraging the family pet to lick their privates, or deliberately letting a dog nuzzle their crotch (as some dogs tend to do anyway!). If you fall into this category, don't beat yourself up about it, or worry that you're a fully-fledged 'pervert'. For reasons of hygiene, it's best to avoid doing it again, but it's not such a terrible thing:

do yourself a favour by putting it down to experience and forgetting all about it.

What's dogging?

Dogging doesn't have anything to do with bestiality. Dogging is what you call it when people do sexual things in a public or semi-public place, while others watch. Both sides get a thrill from doing this. Often the people having sex are in parked cars, whilst those watching spy through the car windows. It usually happens at night, in dark, out of the way places. Sometimes the event is random and unplanned, sometimes it's organised over the internet or by text messaging. The people who enjoy spying on the action are sometimes known as *voyeurs* – they get turned on by secretively watching others engaged in sexual activity. And those who enjoy being watched are sometimes called *exhibitionists* – they get turned on by being seen in sexual positions, or by exposing their genitals. Dogging is generally accepted as a fairly harmless activity. However, voyeurism and exhibitionism both have their darker side. Voyeurs sometimes develop into 'peeping Toms' – people who actively invade others' privacy by spying through their windows to get a glimpse of them naked. And flashers (find out more about them on page 213) are exhibitionists who expose their genitals to people in what is often a disturbing and upsetting way.

What does the word frigid mean?

Some people use this word to describe a girl or woman who doesn't like or want to have sex, and men sometimes use it as an insult – usually when a girl refuses to sleep with them! In the past it was thought that frigidity was an actual medical condition, but it's now known that there's no such thing – how much you want or like sex is just a matter of taste, and there's certainly nothing medically wrong with you if you're not so keen.

178

I'm a boy who likes wearing outrageous clothes. The other day, someone called me a transvestite. What's that?

Transvestism means, literally, cross-dressing: wearing clothes that are typical of the opposite sex. A transvestite is someone who does this, and it doesn't sound like you're one – you choose to wear unusual clothes, not 'girls' clothes.

Transvestism is far more common in boys than in girls (perhaps because it's not considered weird for girls to wear 'boys' clothes' anyway). A boy or man who is a transvestite usually feels comfy and happy when he dresses as a girl, and may also get sexually excited when he does it. Transvestites are usually straight, and don't actually want to *be* girls; they just get a kick – sexual or otherwise – from dressing up. Discovering that you're into cross-dressing can be horribly confusing, and transvestites often suffer in silence and do their dressing up in secret. If you think you might be a transvestite and want to talk about it, the London Lesbian and Gay Switchboard are there to confidentially help and support anyone who needs to consider issues around their gender or sexuality. Call their helpline on 0300 330 0630.

Are transsexuals the same as transvestites?

No, although both transsexuals and transvestites come under the umbrella term *transgender*. Transgender is a difficult word to define because for different people it has slightly different meanings, but basically it describes men and women who don't identify with the 'normal' ideas of what it means to be male, or female.

Transsexuals are people who feel that they were born the wrong sex. They usually fancy people of the same sex as them, feel more comfortable in the clothes of the opposite sex, feel uncomfortable about their bodies and sexual organs, and wish that they actually *were* the opposite gender. This very difficult position often makes them confused and depressed, and some eventually decide that they'd like to have a *sex change*. The proper term for this is *gender reassignment*, and it's a long and difficult process, involving years of counselling and painful surgery.

If you are, or think you might be, transsexual, and you'd like to speak to someone in confidence for support and advice, try the London Lesbian and Gay Switchboard (0300 330 0630), or Childline on 0800 1111.

Part 4

WHEN THINGS DON'T GO TO PLAN

The road to a happy sex life has its fair share of difficulties and pitfalls. We've looked at the risk of STIs and unwanted pregnancies, and the need to use protection every time you have sex. This part of the book deals with all sorts of other potential problems, from the minor to the very serious. You'll find everything you need to know about solving them, avoiding them or – if the worst comes to the worst – picking yourself up and getting back on the road to happiness.

Chapter 10

Physical Problems
With Sex

You can know all there is to know, but no matter how much of an expert you are at sex, you're almost definitely going to have some physical problems at some point – that is, a situation where you feel your tackle lets you down.

When these things happen, the best thing you can do is to relax, and not worry too much about it. Partners – if your lover has problems like these, never laugh at them, or show impatience or scorn. The best thing you can do is to be kind, loving and reassuring, help them to relax, then give it another go together!

These are the most common troubles . . .

Even when I'm excited, I find that my penis goes soft before I get a chance to use it . . .
Many boys, especially when they've first started being sexually active, find it hard to keep their erections. Usually things start off fine, then you go to put a condom on, or try to put your penis inside your partner, and bingo – it goes limp. It can be

very upsetting and frustrating, but the worst thing you can do is drive yourself crazy worrying that there's something horribly wrong with you, because the whole thing is usually caused by worry and nervousness in the first place.

You'll find that this problem usually sorts itself out as you get to know and relax with your partner. One practical solution that's worth a try in the meantime is to grip and firmly squeeze the base of the penis while you're trying to put on the condom or enter your partner. Either you or your partner can do this, and it works by stopping the blood from rushing out of the penis, and therefore keeps it erect. If this doesn't work for you, just take a breather, then start cuddling, kissing and touching each other until your penis is hard again and have another go. If it takes a few tries, who cares? No one ever said that sex had to be quick and immediate to be fun!

If you're unlucky enough to have a partner who seems impatient or disappointed, it's going to be much harder to overcome. It's worth talking to them about how pressurised and upset you feel. If they really can't understand, perhaps it's time to start looking for a new partner!

This problem can also be caused by drinking alcohol. It's sometimes called *brewer's droop*. Sex and alcohol are a bad mix for other reasons too – see page 206 for more on this.

I always come really quickly – like after only a few seconds. Sometimes I don't even manage to hold on until I get inside!
This problem is called *premature ejaculation,* and it's another one that's really common for boys who are just starting to have sex. You can usually put it down to nerves, and most boys find that it happens less and less as time goes on. However, some men continue to suffer from premature ejaculation throughout their lives. Again, an understanding partner is a big help, and there are plenty of things you can both try to sort things out. The simplest is just to relax a

while, then start again. Some boys find that the solution is to have an orgasm deliberately before having sex (by wanking themselves off, or letting their partner wank them or give them a blow job). Either way, if you've already come once, it should be much easier to hold on longer the second time around.

The most important thing is not to let yourself get into a panic – it'll definitely make things worse. If you don't normally suffer from premature ejaculation, but it happens on the off-chance, don't immediately assume that your partner is going to be disappointed by your 'performance'. Many people take their partner's speedy orgasm as a huge compliment – they could flatter themselves that you were *so* excited by the prospect of having sex with them that you couldn't control yourself! Whatever your partner's attitude, they shouldn't have much reason to complain as long as you continue to cuddle and kiss them and give them lots of loving attention, rather than just rolling over and feeling sorry for yourself.

Every time I've tried to have sex, it's been impossible for my partner to get his penis inside me. What's wrong with me?
Usually this is down to the combination of your vagina being too dry, both of you feeling uncomfortable, and no one wanting to force anything too hard in case they hurt themselves or their partner. This can normally be sorted out by taking the pressure off – you don't have to have sex until you're both completely ready. Relax, do what feels comfortable in terms of foreplay and, if you feel ready, try again.

What you're aiming for is to be relaxed enough to feel turned on. In that state, and with your partner giving you lots of loving, sexy attention, without any particular effort on your part you'll produce your natural vaginal juices, which act as a brilliant lubricant and should help your partner's penis slip in easily and comfortably. Alternatively, you could take a short-cut and use some lubricant (for a reminder, flip back to the section about losing your virginity at the end of Chapter 4).

It's also possible that nerves are making you tense up because you're frightened (perhaps unconsciously) that your partner's penis is going to hurt you as it goes in. If this is the case, you might find that you'd be more relaxed if you had more control over what was going on. The easiest way to do that is to have your partner lie on his back when his penis is hard, sit straddled over him, guide his penis to the right place, then gently lower yourself onto it. That way his penis goes in when *you're* ready, as slowly and gently as you want. Give it a try – it's very empowering and it can be a real turn-on for your partner too!

Chapter 11

Getting Pregnant

This chapter is all about pregnancy, and what your options are if you find that you are pregnant. We've included this chapter in the When Things Don't Go To Plan section, because for many teenagers, an unintended pregnancy is a problem. At the same time, we do realise that for some it's a really happy event!

In this chapter you'll find out all about:
- What Happens When You Get Pregnant
- Could You Be Pregnant?
- Doing a Pregnancy Test
- If the Test's Negative . . .
- And If It's Positive . . .
- Keeping the Baby
- Having the Baby Adopted
- Having an Abortion

What Happens When You Get Pregant

Pregnancy happens when a sperm fertilises a ripe egg, which then successfully implants itself into the wall of the womb and begins to grow into a baby. A pregnancy is measured from the first day of your last period and usually lasts between thirty-seven and forty-two weeks – about nine months – when the baby is born. About one in five pregnancies end in miscarriage, where the *embryo*, or unborn baby, dies and is expelled from the body through the vagina. Most miscarriages happen in the first twelve weeks of pregnancy. Sometimes women are unaware that they have had a miscarriage, mistaking it for a heavy period. Miscarriages that happen later into pregnancy can be much more difficult, physically and emotionally.

If you've had sex and not used your contraception properly (eg, forgetting to take your contraception pill, then not using a condom as back-up); if you have not used any contraception; or if your contraception has failed (say a condom splits), then you are at risk of becoming pregnant.

An inescapable fact is that, even if you're using contraception properly, you can *still* become pregnant, because no contraceptive is 100% fail-safe. So as long as you're sexually active, pregnancy is *always* going to be a possibility, however small. That's why, before you start having sex together, you and your partner should discuss and think about two things: contraception and protection against STIs; and what you might do if you accidentally get pregnant. This chapter should help arm you with lots of information about your options.

Emergency Contraception

Remember that if you do have unprotected sex, you still have the chance to prevent pregnancy if you act fast and take the emergency contraceptive pill within seventy two hours, or have an emergency IUD fitted within 5 days (see page 108 for more on this).

Could You Be Pregnant?

The following are signs which might show that you're pregnant.
- Missing a period
- A period that's shorter or lighter than usual
- Weeing frequently
- Tiredness
- Tender breasts
- Nausea, vomiting, tummy cramps
- Going off certain foods

If you've had sex with a boy, and have any of the above symptoms, you might be pregnant. There's only one way to find out for sure, though, and that's to do a pregnancy test.

Doing a Pregnancy Test

If you've had any of the symptoms above, or had unprotected sex without taking emergency contraception, you should start thinking immediately about the fact that you might be pregnant.

This can be a *really* scary possibility, but ignoring it isn't going to make it go away. The sooner you find out what the score is, the better. If you discover you're not pregnant, you can breathe a sigh of relief and get on with your life – making sure that you're ultra-careful about contraception from now on. If you *are* pregnant, you'll have given yourself plenty of time to think things through and to talk to people about what's best for you.

To find out whether you're pregnant or not, you'll need to have a pregnancy test. This means testing a sample of your wee to look for pregnancy hormones. You simply wee on a stick and the stick then shows in a little window whether the hormones are there – often with a coloured line or two. The pregnancy hormones should appear within a day of your missed period, so you can test as soon as that. If you don't have regular periods, or you can't remember when your period is due, do the test three weeks after you've had unprotected sex.

Where Can I Get a Pregnancy Test ?

You can get a free pregnancy test at done at Brook Centres, a young person's clinic, family planning clinics, your own GP, any other GP (registering for family planning services only) and some sexual health (GUM) clinics. This service will be confidential – ie, the doctor or nurse will not tell anyone about your visit or the test. To find your nearest service, call Ask Brook on 0808 802 1234.

You can also do a pregnancy test yourself. If you chose DIY, you'll need to buy a testing kit. These are available from some supermarkets, chemists or pharmacies and usually cost between £5 and £15. They're easy to use, and good if you'd rather do the test in your own home, perhaps with your partner or a friend for moral support.

A word of warning: you might come across adverts on posters and in magazines for 'Pregnancy testing and advisory services'. Although some of the organisations which place these ads are very helpful, others have hidden motives, and if it turns out that you are pregnant, might try to persuade you to do what *they* think is right. Some are very anti-abortion, and could try to put you off getting your pregnancy terminated. Others are actually private abortion specialists, and might try their best to persuade you to have an abortion with them – which might not be the best thing for you, and could turn out to be expensive. Using any of the services listed opposite (Brook Centres, etc) will ensure that you get your test done by someone who only wants what's right for you, and will not persuade you to do anything you're not happy with.

If the Test's Negative . . .

If a pregnancy test is negative, you're almost definitely in the clear. If your period doesn't come within three days, though, you should do another test, just to be sure – negative tests are occasionally wrong.

What you need to do now is review what went wrong with your contraception if it failed, and to organise proper contraception if you weren't using any. See Chapter 5 to look at the options, and talk to a doctor or nurse.

There may still be the mystery of a missing period to solve, now that you know you're not pregnant. Remember that it's natural for periods to be irregular sometimes, but if you're worried about any symptoms you have, visit a doctor and get yourself checked out.

And if it's Positive . . .

If a pregnancy test is positive, it means you're pregnant – positive tests are almost never wrong.

You might have all kinds of feelings – shock, fear, panic, loneliness, guilt and confusion are common. You might also, even while you're feeling all these things, have a sense of pride that you were able to conceive. You might feel absolutely delighted. You might be worrying about what your partner, friends and parents are going to say and do. You might start looking forward to having a baby and imagining what it might be like. And your feelings are likely to keep changing, too – all this is very natural.

At this time, the most important thing is to get all the advice and information you can about your options, to help you decide what you want to do next. As soon as you possibly can, if you're not already there, visit a Brook Centre, a family planning clinic, young person's service, or your GP surgery. A doctor or nurse can listen to how you are feeling, talk through what your options are, and help you to make the decision that's right for you. Brook Centres are particularly helpful, as they can organise for you to speak to a trained counsellor about things if you'd like to – and this counselling service is free and confidential (that means they won't tell anyone what you tell them – unless you say that's OK). You'll find it's much easier to think straight if you've got a rational, adult person to talk to.

Speaking of adults, many girls are surprised at just how helpful and supportive their parents can be, even if they're shocked or annoyed at first. Parents might want to call Parentline, a free, twenty-four-hour helpline for parents, carers and relatives offering information and support on issues such as teenage pregnancy, which is provided by the organisation

Family Lives on 0808 800 2222. If you really can't talk to your parents, you could try a supportive relative or a nice teacher. You need and deserve all the support you can get.

What Are My Options Now?

Your options are fairly basic: you can keep the baby, you can go through with the pregnancy and then have the baby adopted, or you can have an abortion. Even if you're under 16, no one can force you to do anything. It's your choice, even if what you decide is not what your partner or parents want.

If you are able to, it's a very good idea to talk to your partner, and try to discuss these options with him. He may want to share the responsibility of your final choice and support you. He may support you even if he doesn't agree with your decision. He may not want to be involved. Legally, he doesn't have a right to be a part of your final decision, although it's important to remember that it's his baby too.

Keeping the Baby

What happens when you keep the baby?

If you're pregnant and you decide to keep the baby, the first step will be to talk to your GP or a family planning clinic. They will give you advice and information on how to stay healthy while you're pregnant and help you book the relevant appointments for check-ups and scans. A scan looks at your embryo on screen to make sure that it's developing properly. It's very important to have regular health checks during your pregnancy as well, to monitor how you and the baby are getting on. You will need to eat and drink healthily and if you are a smoker or take drugs or alcohol, you will need to stop while you are pregnant.

Support for teenage parents

It can be tough being a teenage parent. You're likely not to have a lot of money, your education may need to be put on hold for a bit, and your social life will probably suffer, as you won't be able to go out with mates as much as before. If you have a partner, you and he may find it difficult to support each other at this time, and you may find yourself going it alone – being a single mum. Most single mums will tell you that it's pretty hard work all round. You will need support. Lots of it. Make sure that, before you make your big decision, you know how much support you can rely on. Will your parents or any other adults be around to advise you on bringing up a baby, and to babysit? Is your partner going to be fully involved, and share the responsibilities of parenting? What help might *he* need? Have you got a place to live, that's big enough for you *and* a baby? What about money? Do you have an income, or will you need to find out about benefits? All these questions seem a lot to deal with on top of the stress of finding out you're pregnant, but you do need to consider them.

However, as well as all the potential difficulties, there's a lot to look forward to as well! You're luckier than older mums because you'll still have lots of energy to run about after your little one, and you'll still be young when they've grown up and left home. You've got lots of time to catch up with your education, and to have a career, and the experience of being a mum can bring all kinds of satisfaction, happiness and new opportunities. In addition, there's plenty of support, advice and help out there for teenage parents. Have a look in the *Parenting* section of Contacts and Resources for some of these.

Having the Baby Adopted

If you have your baby adopted, it means that you go through the pregnancy and birth, then give the baby to adoptive parents, who become his or her legal parents. Giving your baby up for adoption is much less common than it used to be, because being a single mum is much more accepted these days.

The decision to have your baby adopted can be very difficult. There's always the chance that after months of pregnancy, the experience of birth and actually seeing and holding your baby, you might not want to give it up. The good news is that you *can* change your mind up to six weeks after the baby is born. If you decide to go through with the adoption, at least you can rest assured that your baby will be going to an excellent home, where it will be loved and well looked after. So many people want to adopt babies that social services are able to select the very best parents for your child.

The British Association for Adoption and Fostering (BAAF) will be able to give you more detailed advice and information about having your baby adopted, to help you make this difficult decision. Call 020 7421 2652, and look at their website on www.baaf.org.

What happens when you have a baby adopted?

If you are thinking of having your baby adopted, you need to get advice about it as soon as possible. First visit your GP for support and information about your pregnancy, and talk to them, or to a Brook centre or family planning clinic, about your wish to adopt. They will organise for you to see a social worker, either from social services, or from a voluntary adoption agency. This social worker will be able to discuss with you what's involved in an adoption, and will organise the adoption while you're pregnant, taking into account what kind of family you'd like for your baby. However, nothing will be definitely arranged until after the birth.

You are not forced to reveal the father's identity, but the social worker will want, if possible, to contact him and see how he feels about the adoption. You'll need to provide information about you and about your family's health, to pass on to the new parents.

After the birth, and when your baby has settled down with his or her adoptive parents, you will be asked to sign a formal document, the Adoption Order. You cannot give this formal agreement until the baby is at least six weeks old. If you sign the document, this means that the baby's legal parents are now the adopters. Even after this, though, you can still change your mind. However, the court will have to be convinced that it is in the child's best interests to be returned to you. Adoption can sometimes involve continuing contact between the birth parents and the adoptive family, either face to face or by letter.

Support after having your baby adopted

Choosing to have your child adopted is not an easy option. You may feel grief, loss and anger, as well as a sense of relief, and you might need to share your feelings with someone sympathetic. Your social worker, or another adult that you like and trust, should be able to listen to you, or refer you to a counsellor. Look in Resources and Contacts under *Counselling*, too.

Having an Abortion

Having an abortion means choosing to end a pregnancy. Nearly one in four pregnancies in the UK end in abortion, and over half of under-sixteens who become pregnant choose to end their pregnancy in this way.

In England, Scotland and Wales abortion is legal if you are less than twenty-four weeks pregnant. Abortion is not legal in Northern Ireland. An abortion can be granted for two reasons:

• When the doctor believes that to have a baby would damage the woman's mental and physical health more than having an abortion. This means that going ahead with a pregnancy will make her distressed and depressed.

• When there's a real risk that the baby would be born severely disabled.

Most abortions are carried out for the first reason.

It is not necessary to get your parents' consent to have an abortion, even if you're under sixteen. It's your choice. If you *are* under sixteen, however, your doctor is likely to try and involve a parent or another adult, if you'd rather, to provide additional support for you. Legally, the father of the baby doesn't have to consent the abortion, and needn't even know about it. However, it might be helpful to have his support at this time, if that's at all possible.

Abortion isn't an easy decision to make. It's a subject that arouses strong feelings, and it can be hard to talk about. Most people have views on it, for and against, and a few of these people also believe that their view should apply to everyone. If you are considering having an abortion it's important to find out as much as you can about the subject, to discuss it with sympathetic people who understand your options, then to decide for yourself. Surround yourself, if that's possible, with people who are kind and non-judgemental.

What happens when you have an abortion

If you definitely want to end your pregnancy, you'll need to be referred by a doctor to your local hospital or a clinic. Your own GP, a doctor at a local family planning clinic or a Brook centre will be able to do this for you. You can get abortions on the NHS, or at private clinics, such as Marie Stopes. Abortions in private clinics cost around £600, and can be arranged within a few days. For NHS abortions you may wait for up to four weeks.

The majority of abortions are performed in two ways:

• Up to nine weeks into the pregnancy you can take two pills, one taken thirty-six to forty-eight hours after the first. Within four hours after taking the second pill you experience something like a heavy period, and the pregnancy is terminated.

• The second method is surgical and can be performed up to fifteen weeks into the pregnancy. This is known as the 'suction method' and it involves either a general or local anaesthetic. A tube is inserted through your vagina into the womb, and the pregnancy is terminated by suction.

• After fifteen weeks, the method of abortion depends on the stage of pregnancy. That's why it's very important, if you are choosing to have an abortion, to get it organised as soon as possible. That way, you can avoid the distress and discomfort of a later abortion.

Support after an abortion

Physically, you may experience some bleeding for a few days after an abortion, and you might have some discomfort, rather like period pains. Very rarely, women experience severe bleeding or pain, or have raised temperatures or unusual vaginal discharge. If this is the case, you need to contact a doctor as soon as possible, as this means you may have an infection that needs treating.

You will need to see a doctor one to six weeks after the abortion to make sure that all is well.

Emotionally, you may have all kinds of feelings, and no two girls are going to feel exactly the same. Relief is very common – it is often a huge weight off your mind to know that all the stress and upset of an unwanted pregnancy are over. However, you might also feel guilt, sadness and loneliness, and the need to grieve your loss. You may feel that other people don't understand what you've been through. These feelings may come immediately, or they may be triggered later in life. It's always helpful to talk to someone you can trust about difficult feelings. A friend or a relative might be able to listen sympathetically. Otherwise a trained counsellor may be a good idea – Brook centres can organise this, or have a look in Contacts and Resources under *Counselling*.

Chapter 12

Harmful Situations

So far, this book has dealt with *good* sex – that is, sex between people who care about each other and respect each other's needs and boundaries. Unfortunately, despite our best intentions, sex sometimes takes place in situations and within relationships that are not good – that are harmful to us or to our partners. This chapter deals with some of these issues. Understanding more about what's harmful to you should help you towards sexual relationships that are healthy and happy. In this chapter you'll find information about:

- Unhealthy/Abusive Relationships
- Sexual Relationships with Adults
- Exploitation
- Alcohol and Drugs

Unhealthy/Abusive Relationships

What is an unhealthy relationship?

Perhaps it's helpful to agree on what a *healthy* relationship is first. A healthy relationship is one where you feel happy, free, respected and supported by your partner. You are both equal partners – you are, first of all, very good friends to each other.

No one has a perfect relationship, because, after all, humans aren't perfect! Two people are always going to have their own ways of doing things, and their own opinions on stuff, and there are always going to be some things you disagree on, or even clash. One or the other of you is going to be in a bad mood from time to time. And situations or events outside your relationship (such as problems with your family, or at school) may sometimes cause the two of you stress and put a real strain on the relationship. But if there's a good foundation of love, respect and support there for each other, then you're well on the way to a healthy, happy relationship.

As far as sex is concerned, in a good relationship, neither partner feels obliged to do anything they're not comfortable with. If you have sex with your partner, then sex is something that you do because you love each other and it makes you both happy. Experts on sex agree that the best way to have a happy sexual relationship is to find a partner that is first of all your friend, and good sex naturally follows.

Now, what's an *un*healthy relationship? In an unhealthy relationship, there is a lack of all the good things that bring two people together happily. There's a lack of respect, of equality, of trust and support. Instead of feeling good and settled, you feel bad and insecure. Instead of feeling as if you're both equals, one partner seems more powerful than the other, and uses this position to demean and undermine the other. This partner is mean to you, tries to control you, disrespects and abuses you.

Unhealthy relationships involve *abuse* of one kind or another, in varying degrees of severity. They are *abusive relationships*. Both men and women, boys and girls can be abusive partners or victims of abuse. Abusive behaviour can be verbal, emotional, physical or sexual.

Verbal abuse

. . . is when someone threatens you or insults you, calls you nasty names, or perhaps shouts at you all the time to make you feel bad. They may criticise the way you look, or what you wear. They may tell you no one else would want to go out with you.

Emotional abuse

. . . is when someone uses their power to manipulate and control you. You find yourself feeling scared to do something in case it upsets them. Or they might constantly check up on you, and demand to know where you are all the time. They may get angry with you when you don't drop everything for them. They may try and stop you from seeing your friends, from talking to other people or from doing things that you enjoy.

Physical abuse

. . . is when someone hurts you physically in any way – by slapping or hitting, for example. Even just raising a hand to you, when they're angry, like he or she is about to hit you – this is physical abuse.

Sexual abuse

. . . is when someone forces you into sexual activity that you don't want or threatens you if you don't have sexual contact with them. This may involve trying to force you to go further than you want. You can read more about sexual abuse in Chapter 13.

All these kinds of abuse are very serious and can be very damaging. If you are a victim of *any* abuse, it's really important to remember that you have done nothing wrong. You need the right support to make sure that you are OK and that the abuse does not continue.

If you have experienced any form of abuse, it can be very difficult to talk about. You may feel worried about what might happen if you speak out, and you may be afraid that no one will believe you. Perhaps your partner threatens you with violence if you tell anyone.

It's very important not to let your fears stop you from getting help. Your truth will always be believed. You could tell a trusted friend, teacher or relative about what's going on so they can help make sure you're safe. If you'd rather speak to a stranger about what's going on you could try Childline, twenty four hours a day, on 0800 1111. Youth Access can give you advice about counselling and put you in touch with your nearest young person's counselling service. Phone them on 020 8772 9900 or look online: www.youthaccess.org.uk

If you are in immediate danger, you should call the police.

For relationship problems that are a little less serious, Relate is an organisation that counsels couples together – phone 0300 100 1234 for more information, or look at www.relate.org.uk.

Sexual Relationships With Adults

When we say 'adult', we mean someone over eighteen.

It can sometimes be traumatic enough when people of your own age start noticing you in a sexual way, but it's even stranger and scarier when it's an adult showing a sexual interest in you. If you are flattered by adult attention, or attracted to an adult who is interested in you, you're looking at a potentially dangerous situation – emotionally and legally.

Don't kid yourself that you could cope with any kind of sexual relationship with an adult, no matter how mature, confident and savvy you are. These relationships are almost always damaging for the younger person. However, it's not *you* that would be the problem, it's them.

This is because adults hold a position of power over children and young adults. This power imbalance means that a relationship between an adult and a young person is open to manipulation and abuse.

Some teenagers think that because they give their *consent* to be in a sexual relationship with an adult, that the adult is not breaking the law. Consent is a legal term, and in this context it means agreeing to have sex, without being forced to. They are wrong about this. Any adult who has *any* sexual contact (and this can just mean touching genitals) with someone under the age of sixteen is committing a crime, regardless of whether the young person agreed to it or not. And for this crime they can expect a prison sentence.

For an adult in a position of authority over young people (eg, teachers, youth leaders, sports coaches, etc) the crime is viewed even more seriously. Adults in these positions are expected to control any urges they have, and not to use their power to manipulate and betray the children they are caring for. If they have *any* sexual contact with any under-eighteens (never mind under-sixteens) whether they consent to sex or not, they are committing a crime known as 'abuse of trust' and they can expect a heavy prison sentence.

If an under-sixteen consents to have a sexual relationship with an adult who is *not* in a position of authority over them (for example, your friend's twenty-year-old brother or sister), this adult is still committing a crime.

Most seriously of all, if an adult has sex with an under-thirteen year old, even if the child has consented to it or if the adult *thinks* they have consented to it, that adult will be imprisoned for life.

Exploitation

Sexual exploitation is when a young person is used for sex by someone who promises them something in return. This person may pay you for sex with them, or for sex with other people. The payment may be money, gifts or just somewhere to stay. What's happening here is that you are being turned into a prostitute. This is sexual exploitation, and it is very dangerous, illegal and always wrong.

Sometimes the person who is exploiting you tells you they loves you. They may buy you presents and make you feel special by paying you lots of attention. But *anyone* who pays you for sex, or allows other people to have sex with you, is exploiting you and committing a very serious crime.

Sexual exploitation can happen to any young person – girls and boys. If you are being sexually exploited, it's very important to remember that you have done nothing wrong. You may feel frightened and helpless and unable to change the situation. But you can come out of it, and many people are there to support you. If you are worried that you, or someone else is being sexually exploited, call Childline on 0800 1111 or the NSPCC's Child Protection helpline on 0808 800 5000. Both are free, open twenty-four hours a day, and you don't have to say who you are. You can also call your local police – look them up in the phone book or online.

Alcohol and Drugs

Alcohol and Sex

- Did you know that after drinking alcohol, one in seven sixteen to twenty four year olds have had unprotected sex?
- That one in five have had sex that they regretted?
- That one in ten have been unable to remember if they even *had* sex the night before?
- That 60% of young women who are infected with a sexually transmitted infection say they were under the influence of alcohol when they had sex with the infected person?
- That four out of ten thirteen and fourteen year olds were drunk or high on other drugs when they lost their virginity?
- That alcohol is a factor in many rapes and sexual assaults, with the attacker, victim or both having been drinking?

These scary facts demonstrate some of the effects that alcohol has on us. Even a couple of alcoholic drinks can make you:

Feel uninhibited, relaxed and horny (feeling sexual desire).

Unable to think clearly.

Have sex with someone you don't like much, or go further sexually than you want to.

Be less likely to use contraception and condoms, so risk an STI or an unintended pregnancy.

Take other dangerous risks, like accepting lifts from strangers.

It's also worth mentioning that having sex with someone who is incapacitated due to alcohol (passed out or too drunk to think clearly) is against the law.

Alcohol and Us

Sex and alcohol are very strongly linked in our culture. For many people, young and old, alcohol is an important part of socialising with friends, and of relaxing and enjoying ourselves before sex. The problem is that although we can often have a good time when we've had a couple of drinks, things can easily go wrong and the situation can become unsafe and unpleasant at best, and downright dangerous and life-threatening at worst.

Staying Safe With Alcohol

The fact that alcohol is so very much part of our social lives, and so readily available, means that it can be difficult to drink in moderation or to steer clear of it altogether. Peer pressure (mentioned on pages 52-53) means that many of us feel obliged to drink to be part of the group, even if we don't like it much. Because we're not used to going out with our friends and *not* drinking, we wonder if we'll enjoy ourselves if we're sober. And if everyone's drinking, we feel that we should too.

Remember, if you don't enjoy drinking alcohol, then your friends should accept your decision not to. You'll probably find that some of them are not happy with this at first – they may take the piss, or try to make you change your mind. After a while, though, they'll get used to the fact and stop making a big deal of it. And the truth is, you can have just as good a time, whatever you're doing, if you're sober!

For those who *do* want to drink alcohol, here are some tips on staying safe and happy:

Look after your friends

If you're going out for the night and you know that you'll all be drinking, arrange for one of you to stay sober. Not just to drive people back home, but to make sure everyone's OK throughout the evening.

Set your boundaries

If you're out with your partner, with someone new, or with your mates, let them know how much you intend to drink that evening, and don't drink more than that. The idea is that you don't get drunk – perhaps you decide on one or two drinks only. You keep your wits about you and stop at your limit, and your partner or mates are there to remind you if you don't. This is especially important if you're out on a first date, because you don't want to do anything embarrassing or unsafe in that situation.

Watch your drinks

In the next chapter, we mention the danger of drinks spiked with 'date rape' drugs. Sometimes people spike our drinks with extra alcohol too, or ask a barperson to do so, in order to make us drunk enough to have sex with them. To make sure neither of these things happen, always watch while your drink is being poured. And if you are going to put your drink down, only leave it with someone you know very well. Don't leave your drink unattended and don't accept drinks from people you don't know.

See what you're drinking

It's a good idea to stick to drinks where you can *see* what you're drinking, like lager or cider, rather than things like cocktails, where you can't clearly tell what or how much you're drinking and you might end up with more than you bargained for.

Alternate with soft drinks

Try drinking a soft drink between every alcoholic drink. This means you'll drink less alcohol *and* be better hydrated, so you'll have less of a hangover the next morning!

Know how you'll get home

Before you go out, plan how you'll get home again, safely – perhaps this is means organising a lift, arranging to walk home with a friend, looking up bus times, or making sure you have the money for a taxi. If you take any taxi, it has to be a licenced vehicle. Don't ever take an unlicensed minicab, or accept a lift from a stranger.

Know who you will call if you need help

Before you step out of the door, check that your mobile is topped up and the battery's full. You also need to have the number of someone who can come and help if something goes wrong. It can be scary to call a parent or a carer and admit you're drunk and need help, but even if they're angry they will want to make sure you're safe. If the worst comes to the worst, call the police. They will make sure that you are OK and will get you home safely.

If you need help or information about alcohol or alcohol-related issues, call Drinkline on 0800 917 8282, or click on *alcohol and drugs* on www.thesite.org, a really handy website run by YouthNet UK.

Drugs and Sex

All drugs involve risks and side-effects. But there are also some special risks in combining drugs and sex that you should know about. Drugs can lead you to taking the same kind of risks as alcohol, because they may make you feel less inhibited, less sensitive to pain, or less able to take control of

the situation you're in. So, if you're on drugs, you're more likely to . . .
- have sex that you did not consent to
- have unprotected sex and put yourself at risk of pregnancy or an STI
- have sex that hurts you
- not be able to remember the sex you had.

Different drugs do different things to your body and mind. They can be very dangerous. If you're going to take them, you have to understand what you're doing. You can find out more about drugs on the Frank website (www.talktofrank.co.uk) or call them on 0800 776600.

Chapter 13

When You Don't Want Sex

It's a grim reality that people are sometimes forced to have sex against their wishes. This can happen in all kind of situations, and to all kinds of people – young people, adults, men, women and children, gays and straights. This chapter tells you something about what these situations might be, how best to deal with them, and how to recover from them.

The two most important things to remember are these:

1) In any situation where you have sex without agreeing to it, or where you are frightened into agreeing to it, you are not to blame for it happening.

2) Tell someone about it to make sure that it doesn't happen again.

In this chapter we look at:
• Sexual Harassment
• Sexual Abuse
• Sexual Assault
• Rape
• Staying Safe

Sexual Harrassment

We mentioned sexual harassment in Chapter 3, which was all about attitudes to sex.

What is sexual harassment?

Sexual harassment is intimidation, bullying or coercion of a sexual nature. Coercion here means trying to make you do something sexual against your will. Sexual harassment can take place anywhere, and the harasser can be anyone – a fellow pupil at school, a stranger, an adult or a young person. They can be either male or female, an individual or a group. The harasser is usually in a position of power over the victim – perhaps because he or she is part of a gang and the victim is alone, perhaps because they are physically stronger than the victim, perhaps because they are an adult and you are under 16. The victim does not have to be the person directly targeted by the harasser, but can be anyone who finds the harasser's behaviour intimidating and upsetting. Sometimes the harasser is unaware that his or her behaviour is upsetting.

Examples of sexual harassment might be:

• being the target of a gang who persistently call out offensive sexual insults

• being propositioned for sex in insulting or degrading ways

• being asked about your sex life

• having pornographic images thrust in front of you to see your reaction.

If anything like this happens to you, and it upsets, scares or just severely irritates you, it's sexual harassment and it needs to be taken seriously by those in charge. It's not your fault that it's happening, and it needs to be stopped. This is a very serious form of bullying.

What to do if you're sexually harassed

You need to report the offender or offenders to a teacher, a superior at work or anyone else in a higher position of authority than the person or gang who is harassing you.

Many schools have anti-bullying policies, but even if yours doesn't, tell a teacher. Teachers need to know what's happening so they can sort it out and stop it. To talk or get advice, ring Childline on 0800 1111. You could also look online at Kidscape, the anti-bullying organisation, which has lots of useful information and advice on its website: www.kidscape.org.uk. If you can do this, you're not just protecting yourself, but anyone else who is being harassed.

Flashers

Flashers are people (usually men) who get a sexual kick from exposing their genitals to people (usually women). They very rarely touch their victims, so in this situation you are generally safe, however, it can be a shocking confrontation, and may leave you feeling abused in some way.

If you are flashed at, try not to show any reaction, but do move away from the flasher. Don't say anything to him – giving a reaction encourages him in his fantasy that you secretly enjoyed it.

Being flashed at doesn't bother everyone – to some people it can seem quite funny and harmless – but if it ever happens to you, it's important to tell an adult, and then the police. Flashers are *not* harmless. They usually start this negative sexual behaviour as teenagers, and unless they are treated as soon as possible, it's likely that they'll go on to commit more serious sexual crimes in the future.

Sexual Abuse

We mentioned a little about sexual abuse within relationships in the last chapter.

What is sexual abuse?

Sexual abuse is when someone is used sexually by an adult or another young person. It means being pressurised, forced or tricked into taking part in any kind of sexual activity. This can include kissing, touching genitals or breasts, sexual intercourse or oral sex. Making someone look at pornographic magazines, films or other people engaged in sexual activity is also sexual abuse. Sexual abuse doesn't just happen to children and young people – a person of any age, and from either sex, can be sexually abused, even babies and the elderly.

Who sexually abuses people?

Sex abusers can come from any kind of background, race or religion, and can be male or female. They are not always adults – a young person might sexually abuse someone their own age. Usually the sex abuser is in a position of power over the victim – they could be someone in authority, like a teacher, babysitter or a parent. Or they might simply be bigger and stronger than you – like an older sibling, or someone in the class above you at school.

Sex abusers are usually known to the victim, which means that they may be a family member or a family friend – they could be someone that you love and trust. Sexual abuse by a family member (for example a parent or a sibling) is also called *incest*. Child sex abusers are often called *paedophiles* or *sex offenders*, especially when they are not family members.

214

How do sex abusers operate?

They may operate alone, or as an organised group. They sometimes prefer children of a particular age, sex, physical type or ethnic background.

These people go to great lengths to get close to and win your trust. For example, they may choose employment that brings them into contact with young people, and they may pretend to be children or teenagers in internet chatrooms. They may buy their victims presents and pay them a lot of attention before they abuse them, and sometimes they may show them pornography. This is called *grooming*, and it's designed to get you to do as they say.

After the abuse, they may pressurise you very strongly to keep it secret. They often target lonely children, or make their victims hurt younger children, so that they can use this to make them feel guilty, and not to tell. Commonly, they tell their victims that it's *their* fault the abuse is happening – that you gave them the come-on, that you wanted it, and that if you tell anyone, they will reveal this. They say that no one will believe you, or that you will cause trouble, break up the family, make people ill. Confusingly, your body often responds sexually to touch and stimulation, even though you hate what's going on. This can make you feel very guilty, and believe that the abuser must be right when he or she says you are enjoying it.

The effects of sexual abuse

It is very difficult to cope with the experience of sexual abuse. This is especially true if the abuser is a parent or close family member, or if the abuse has continued for a long time, or is particularly violent or frightening. You might find yourself suffering from depression, eating disorders, alcohol or drug addiction, and have problems sustaining trusting and loving relationships. You may not be able to admit to yourself that the abuse even happened – because it is so distressing to consider. So you suffer in silence, without being clear about why.

However, many, many victims of sexual abuse recover from their experience, and go on to lead happy lives *and* have good, loving relationships. These days there is a lot of support for you, and a lot more awareness of the extent and the effects of sexual abuse. You deserve and will find the support and kindness that you need. Counselling, where you talk to a sympathetic professional about your experiences, can be a really positive way to start the process of healing. Youth Access can give you advice about counselling and put you in touch with your nearest young person's counselling service. Call 020 8772 9900 (open Monday-Friday, 9am-1pm and 2pm-5.30pm) or look online: www.youthaccess.org.uk

What to do if you have been sexually abused

The abuser will have told you that the abuse is your fault, that you wanted it, that if you tell, you will cause trouble, and that no one will believe you. It is NEVER someone's fault if they have been sexually abused. You have done NOTHING wrong, and people WILL believe your story. **You must tell someone** so that the abuse can be stopped immediately.

You will probably feel very frightened about what will happen, but you must tell someone. This will be especially hard for you if the abuser is a close family member, or someone you love, but you are being harmed, and your safety has to come first.

• Tell an adult that you trust, and if they don't believe you, tell another. Keep telling people until you find someone who does believe you.

• Or talk to a friend first, and ask him/her to come with you to tell an adult.

• If you find it difficult to speak about the abuse, write it down and give it to the person you'd like to help you, perhaps with the support of your friend.

• If none of the adults are helpful, look up 'police' or your borough council online or in the phone book, call them and tell the switchboard that you'd like to speak to someone about child abuse. You can report what's happened, or you can remain anonymous and get advice from them.

• If you just want to talk to someone about the abuse, find out what will happen if you report it and obtain information and counselling, phone the NSPCC Child Protection Helpline on 0808 800 5000. It's open twenty-four hours a day, it's free, and you don't have to say who you are.

Sometimes you only recognise and properly recall the truth of your own sexual abuse years after it happened. However, it's never too late to seek help for yourself, and to report the abuser, if you choose to.

Sexual Assault

What is sexual assault?
When someone gropes or touches you sexually without your permission, whether they are an adult or someone your own age, they are committing a *sexual assault*. The person committing the assault and their victim might be either male or female. This is a criminal offence, which means that the person who does so may be prosecuted by the police.

What to do if you are sexually assaulted
As with sexual harassment, if you have been sexually assaulted

you need to tell teachers or others in authority what has happened, and the police will probably need to be informed too, as soon as possible after the event.

The police will always take the ages of the people involved into account. For example, sexual assault of a person under thirteen by someone over eighteen carries a sentence of up to fourteen years in prison. For a minor offence (like inappropriate touching), where both of you are under sixteen, the police would be more likely to refer the case to social services. If it happened at school, the police may suggest that the school deals with it. Whatever the situation, you can be sure that the police would be sympathetic towards you.

Rape

What is rape?
Having sex should always be your own decision, and it is only legal if you have given your consent. If anyone makes you have sex against your wishes, they are committing a rape. Rape occurs when a man intentionally penetrates the mouth, vagina or anus with his penis, without your consent. Serious sexual assault is classed together with rape – this involves penetration of the mouth, vagina or anus with a part of the body or an object.

What kind of people rape, and why? Here are some myths about rape that help explain a few facts.

Eight myths about rape

All rapists are strangers
In over 90% of cases, the people who commit rape are known to their victims. They are often an acquaintance, a friend, a

partner, or a former lover. Around half of rapes happen in the victim or the attacker's home. So-called 'Date rape' and 'Aquaintance rape' often fall into this category (see page 220 for more on this).

Rape happens because men are unable to control their sexual urges.
The vast majority of men manage to control their sexual urges very well, as do women. Rape is not about sexual desire, but about power, violence and dominance over another person. In fact, many rapists struggle to maintain an erection during their attacks.

The victim was raped because of the way he or she was dancing, or the way they dressed.
Rape is rape, and can only be blamed on the perpetrator. As long as we don't hurt others, we all have the right to dress and behave as we please, to wear revealing clothes and to express ourselves through activities like dancing. And we have the right to remain safe. Women, children and men of all ages (including babies and the elderly) can be rape victims – not just attractive young women and men.

People who rape boys and men are gay.
Men who rape other men are not necessarily gay or bisexual themselves. They may even be married to women.

All rape victims have injuries.
Not all rapes involve outright violence. For example, someone who is raped while asleep or out of it on drugs or alcohol may have no bruises or cuts.

A rape victim has to say no to show that they have not consented to rape.
Sometimes women are too terrified to struggle and protest during rape. This does not mean that they agreed to have sex. The police know that this is the case.

The police won't believe me.
Police training has improved hugely in this area. You can expect to be taken seriously and treated with sensitivity.

You can only report rape to the police.
You can go to your local Sexual Assault Referral Centre (SARC) and report the rape there, if you'd rather go to a police station. See page 223) for more about SARCs.

Date and Acquaintance Rape

Both these terms are used to describe rape that happens with someone you already know. With date rape, you choose to go on a date with someone and are then raped. Attackers could be your current partner, a first-time date, an ex-partner, someone you met on the internet or a pen-pal. With acquaintance rape, you are raped by someone you know, who is not a close friend – this could be your friend's partner, a teacher, doctor or youth worker.

The terms 'date rape' and 'acquaintance rape' can be dangerous because they make the crime of rape seem less serious, and imply that because you know the attacker, you may share some of the blame. Rape is always a very serious crime, and the perpetrator is always to blame. If you have been raped in these circumstances, you are likely to feel all the same emotions and trauma that you would if you were raped by a stranger.

Drug Rape or DFSA
(Drug Facilitated Sexual Abuse)

'Drug rape' is the label given by the media to the recent rise in rapes that take place when a rapist gives you a drug (usually Rohypnol or GHB) in a social setting such as a party, a nightclub, pub or bar. The rapist may be known, or unknown to you. The drugs are usually slipped into your drink without your knowledge.

The effect of these drugs is to make you physically helpless and unaware of what is happening during the assault. Memories of the rape may or may not resurface later. After the rape, you may feel extreme fear and an 'out of control' sensation, particularly if you cannot clearly remember what happened. You may have physical injuries, but will be unaware of them immediately or unaware of how they came about. The drugs leave the system about 48 hours after they're taken, which often means that when the memory of the rape returns, there's no evidence that you were given the drug.

This kind of rape is growing worldwide. The Roofie Foundation, a UK charity that helps victims of drug rape, estimate that ten thousand people have phoned their helpline to report drug rapes since the charity was set up in 1996. And they reckon that many, many more have experienced drug rape and not reported the crime.

If you wake up in a strange place, or even at home, with your underwear scattered around, sore genitals and other evidence of sex, you may have been drugged and raped or assaulted. Follow the advice given under *What to do if you've been or raped or sexually assaulted,* and remember, if you can, to take a urine sample, in a clean container with a screw top, before all evidence of the drug leaves your body in around two days' time. This could be very important in finding out what happened, whether or not you decide to report the crime.

The Effects of Rape

The experience of rape or sexual assault is extremely traumatic. Common immediate feelings are shock, denial, disbelief and a determination to carry on with life as if nothing has happened. Later you might experience shame, anger, humiliation and depression. In the longer term you may find it hard to sleep, have nightmares and suffer flashbacks. You may find it hard to have anyone near you.

Remember that you have nothing to hide or be ashamed of. Telling someone is very, very important, and once you have taken that first step, you're on your way to surviving the experience. The organisation Rape Crisis is there to assist rape victims initially and in the long term, with advice, support, and information. They can help you find a trained counsellor too. Find them at www.rapecrisis.org.uk, free helpline 0808 802 9999.

What To Do If You've Been Raped or Sexually Assaulted

If you've been raped or sexually assaulted, you'll probably be in a state of shock and may not be able to think very clearly. The very first thing to remember is that, whatever happened and however you feel, you are not to blame for being raped and there was nothing you could have done to prevent the assault. Now you need to get to a safe place as soon as you can, preferably home. Here are some ideas for what you to do next.

1) Speak to a friend, and/or an adult that you trust about what has happened.

2) Getting medical attention is a priority. Go with your friend or the adult to a clinic to get advice on STIs and emergency contraceptives, as you may have had unprotected sex. You might also have other injuries that need dealing with. GPs

and hospitals will treat you confidentially and will not pressurise you to report the incident if you don't want to. Sexual Assault Referral Centres (SARCs) specialise in looking after all aspects of care for rape and assault victims. They're open twenty four hours a day and employ specially trained, experienced professionals who provide medical care, contraceptive advice and treatment and forensic examination (this means that they collect and analyse proof of your rape or sexual assault, should you wish to report the incident). They will help and support you through the initial trauma and will also assist you throughout the criminal justice process, if you choose to press charges against the rapist. Contact NHS Direct on 0845 4647 or www.nhsdirect.uk to find your nearest SARC.

If you decide to go to the police:

• Although you'll really want to, try not to wash or shower, as forensic evidence might be vital to prove your case. Don't worry if you *have* washed, it's likely that there will still be evidence.

• Keep any clothes you were wearing safe and unwashed, so you can give them to the police. Keep them even if you don't go to the police, in case you change your mind.

• Ask your friend and/or the adult to accompany you to the police station.

• A specially trained officer will talk to you, and be guided by your wishes. Don't worry if you're not sure what happened. The police are there to help you, and you don't have to go to court if you don't want to.

The Victim Support helpline (0845 30 30 900) offers free and confidential help for victims of crime and their families.

If you've been raped or sexually assaulted, no one but those you choose to tell will know. It's a criminal offence for anyone to publish your name, photo or any other details that might identify you.

Staying Safe

Looking after yourself is very important. Here are some suggestions to minimise the risk of anything happening to you when you're out and about. ALWAYS be careful, but do be reassured that violent crimes are still pretty rare.

Avoiding Drug Rape

To have a great, safe night out, try to follow all the safety tips outlined in the section on alcohol on page 206). Plus:

When you're out:
- Don't share drinks with others.
- Don't accept drinks from people you don't trust.
- Never leave a drink unattended for any reason, if you do, don't drink from it again.
- Ask for/buy drinks in bottles – they are harder to slip the drug into – and keep your thumb over the top.

Your drink may have been spiked by drugs if:
- You feel strange, sick or really drunk after a couple of alcoholic drinks.
- You feel this way after drinking only non-alcoholic drinks – tea, coffee, fruit juice, etc.

If you think your drink's been spiked:
- Get to a place of safety. Tell a friend you know and trust completely how you're feeling and ask them to get you home as soon as possible.
- Once home, ask the friend to stay with you and make sure you're OK till the drug is out of your system. Lie down.

• If you're alone or with a stranger, ask the owner of the pub/bar/club you're in to take you somewhere safe (like the office) and to phone your parents or for a taxi to take you home.

• NEVER let a stranger or acquaintance offer to help you or take you anywhere – they could be the rapist.

Street Safety

After a night out, get home as safely and as quickly as possible. Here are some tips:

• Plan ahead, and think about how you're going to get home. Walking with a friend? Organising a lift? Finding bus or train times?

• Don't walk by yourself. If possible, stick with mates.

• If you're out in a group, stick together and don't let anyone walk home alone.

• Walk confidently and stick to well-lit streets where there are people around. Avoid quiet or badly-lit alleyways, subways or isolated car parks.

• Trust your instincts – they're there to help you.

• Don't chat on your mobile or wear headphones – you need to be aware of your surroundings.

• Avoid passing stationary cars with their engines running and people sitting in them.

• If a car pulls up next to you, turn around and run in the other direction – you can turn faster than a car.

• In buses or trains, sit as close to the driver as you can, and move if you feel uncomfortable.

• If you think you are being followed, head into a shop or towards people.

• Yell and make lots of noise to attract attention if someone threatens you. Run away if you can.

• Give away your bag, purse and mobile rather than fighting. Your safety is much more important.

Dating Safely

How to have a safe date:

• Give details of where you're going, who you're meeting and when you expect to return to your parents, or a trusted friend.

• Take a friend with you on your first date. Arrange to give them a signal to leave if and when you feel comfortable enough with your date.

• Arrange your first few dates in a busy, public place, preferably in the daytime, until you get to know them and feel comfortable.

• Don't be completely alone with your date, go back to their place or accept a lift from them until you know them well.

• Trust your instincts – they're usually right. If someone makes you feel nervous or uneasy, even if you can't put your finger on why – leave immediately and don't see them again.

Internet Safety

Chatrooms are fun and safe if you follow some simple rules.

• Never give out personal details such as your name, address, phone number or photo.

• Choose a nickname to use in chatrooms – never use your real name.

• Some adults and older teenagers use chat rooms to groom kids, by telling you things they think you want to hear. Then they try to get you to do what they want. Remember that not everyone is who they say they are. If you are worried or suspicious about anything, go with your instincts, and tell an adult you trust – like a parent or a teacher you can rely on.

• Tell this adult if you come across anything on the

internet that scares or upsets you, like pornography and threatening or offensive language.

• It's a very bad idea to meet up with anyone you've met online as it can be dangerous. If you do, make sure that you tell your parents, or another adult that you trust, take someone with you – an adult, if you can – meet in a busy place, and don't forget your mobile.

Only The Beginning

Whether you've read the book all the way through in one sitting (you'll be pretty exhausted if so!), taken your time and worked your way through, chapter by chapter, or just dipped in and out and looked at the bits that interested you the most, you'll hopefully have a clearer idea about sex than you did before. The last few chapters make pretty grim reading, and perhaps you found the information about STIs and pregnancy scary too – these *are* scary subjects. Do try to remember, though, that the kind of violent crimes we've just been talking about don't happen very often, especially if you look after yourself and stay safe. Likewise, as long as you are careful to practise safe sex, you're very unlikely to experience unintended pregnancies and STIs.

Once safety's taken care of, and if you fancy it, you're free to enjoy all the wonders of sex with someone that you care about and trust! What could be better? Here's to a healthy, happy sex life.

Contacts and Resources

If you have any questions, or feel you need advice, information or support, here are a list of useful websites and helplines that should be able to help you. Many of them have already been mentioned in the book. If you call them, remember it's helpful to have a pen and paper handy to jot down notes.

Phone numbers starting 0800 and 0808 are free to call from a BT landline and won't show up on phone bills. However, they aren't free from most mobiles, and may appear on the bill. Phone numbers starting 0845 and 0300 are charged at local (cheap) rates from landlines, and will appear on the bill.

Adoption

British Association for Adoption and Fostering (BAAF) provide information and publications about adoption and fostering.

Tel: 020 7421 2652 (open Monday-Friday, 9am-1pm)

www.baaf.org

Alcohol and Drugs

Drinkline is staffed by trained counsellors and offers free information, help and support to people with drink problems and to their families.

Tel: 0800 917 8282 (open Monday-Friday, 9am-11pm)

Frank offers confidential advice and support for young people and their parents on drug problems.

Text: 82111
Tel: 0800 776 600 (open 24/7)
Email: frank@talktofrank.com
www.talktofrank.com

Bullying

Kidscape works to prevent bullying and child abuse. The website is full of anti-bullying tips and advice, and information on child abuse.

The helpline is for the parents of bullied children – children are advised to phone Childline (see page 232).

Helpline: 08451 205 204 (open Monday-Thursday, 10am-4pm)
www.kidscape.org.uk

Counselling

Relate organise counselling for couples who are having difficulties in their relationships. They provide face-to-face, phone and online counselling services.

Tel: 0300 100 1234
www.relate.org.uk

Samaritans help by listening supportively and nonjudgmentally to anyone who is going through a difficult time. As well as a 24-hour phoneline, you can email them, find your local branch from the website to talk to someone face to face, or write a letter to Chris, PO Box 9090, Stirling FK8 2SA.

Tel: 08457 90 90 90 (24/7)
Email: jo@samaritans.org
www.samaritans.org

Youth Access can give you advice about counselling and put you in touch with your nearest young person's counselling service.

Tel: 020 8772 9900 (open Monday-Friday, 9am-1pm and 2pm-5.30pm)
www.youthaccess.org.uk

Health

NHS Direct provides medical advice both over the phone and online, through a program where you key in your symptoms to find out what condition you have and where to go for treatment.

Tel: 0845 4647 (24/7)
www.nhsdirect.nhs.uk

Law

The Children's Legal Centre is a charity concerned with the laws affecting children. They provide legal advice, information and representation for children and young people through their advice line and website.

The Child Law Advice Line: 0808 8020 008 (Monday-Friday, 9am-5pm)
www.children'slegalcentre.com

Lesbian, Gay and Transgender Issues

London Lesbian and Gay Switchboard provides information, support and referral services for lesbians, gay men, bisexual and trans people and anyone who needs to consider issues around their sexuality. Their helpline is staffed by trained volunteers who are all gay, lesbian or bisexual.
Tel: 0300 330 0630 (daily, 10am-11pm)
www.llgs.org.uk

Life Problems / General

Childline is a free, confidential helpline for children to phone if they are worried about anything. The website has information and advice on all kinds of topics that affect children.
Tel: 0800 1111 (24/7)
www.childline.org.uk

The Muslim Community Helpline provides a confidential, non-judgemental listening and emotional support service for the UK Muslim community. Their website also contains useful links.
Tel: 020 8904 8193 and 020 8908 6715 (Monday-Friday 10am-1pm)
www.muslimcommunityhelpline.org.uk

The *NSPCC* campaigns to end cruelty to children. They provide free and confidential help and advice for adults who are concerned about children's welfare. Children wanting help and advice are directed to Childline – see details above.

Tel: 0808 800 5000 (24/7)

Text: 88858

Email: help@nspcc.org.uk

www.nspcc.org.uk

Victim Support offer a free and confidential support line for victims of crime, witnesses and their families and friends.

Supportline: 0845 30 30 900 (9am-9pm Monday-Friday; 9am-7pm weekends; 9am-5pm bank holidays)

www.victimsupport.com

YouthNet UK is an organisation that provides online support, guidance and advice for young adults, on subjects like sex, drugs, alcohol, health, law, and much more. They have a handy online answering service, and a very comprehensive website.

www.thesite.org

Parenting

Family Lives supports families by providing advice, directing them towards local services, and giving parents support and information about issues that might affect their children, such as drugs, truancy, bullying and mental health problems.

Parentline: 0808 800 2222 (24/7)

www.familylives.org.uk

Gingerbread is an organisation which provides free help and information on benefits, money, housing and childcare to single parents or young women who are pregnant and living with a parent.

Helpline: 0808 802 0925 (Mondays 10am-6pm; Tues/Thurs/Fri 10am-4pm; Wednesdays 10am-1pm and 5pm-7pm)

www.gingerbread.org.uk

Maternity Action provides good information about mothers' employment rights and entitlement to benefits, via their confidential helpline and free leaflets.

Advice line: 0845 600 8533 (Wednesdays 5pm-9pm; Thursdays 12-4pm; Fridays 8am-12noon)

www.maternityaction.org.uk

Tommy's is a charity which helps people have healthy pregnancies. They've written a Young Woman's Guide to Pregnancy specifically for women under 20, which includes the real pregnancy experiences of young mums. It's available free to teenagers through the Tommy's website: www.tommys.org.

Personal Safety

Rape Crisis has centres across the UK and Ireland and offers free telephone advice, information and counselling for women and girls who have suffered a sex attack recently or in the past. For your local branch, look at their website, or call their helpline.

0808 802 9999 (24/7)

www.rapecrisis.org.uk

Survivors UK is dedicated to providing support, counselling and advice for boys and men who have been raped or assaulted.

Helpline: 0845 122 1201 (Mondays and Tuesdays 7pm-9.30pm; Thursdays 12noon-2.30pm)
www.survivorsuk.org

Sexual Health / Contraception / Unplanned Pregnancy

bpas (British Pregnancy Advisory Service) is a charity with 33 branches around the country, which offers pregnancy testing, emergency contraception and abortion for a fee.

Tel: 08457 30 40 30 (Monday-Friday 8am-9pm; Saturday 8.30am-6pm; Sunday 9.30am-2.30pm)

Brook Advisory are an organisation who provide the under-25s with free, confidential advice on all aspects of sexual health, contraception, pregnancy and relationships, through their website and helpline. They also run a large number of clinics around the UK called Brook Centres, and can direct you to other helpful services locally.

Ask Brook: 0808 802 1234 (Monday-Friday 9am-5pm)
www.brook.org.uk

The fpa (Family Planning Association) is a sexual health charity that gives information, support and advice on sexual health, contraceptives, sex and relationships. They have an emailing service called Ask WES, which you can access from the website.

fpa Sexual Health Helpline: England – 0845 122 8690 (Monday-Friday, 9am-6pm); Northern Ireland – 0845 122 8687 (Monday-Friday, 9am-5pm)

www.fpa.org.uk

The Herpes Virus Association exists to help those with genital herpes to help themselves, with helpful tips on how to cope with the infection, and how to avoid spreading it.

Helpline: 0845 123 2305. If the phone isn't answered, the answermachine message will tell you what time to phone to speak to someone.

www.herpes.org.uk

Marie Stopes is a charity which, for a fee, offers help with contraception, sexual health and abortion. They have clinics all over the country. To find the nearest one to you, check you their website.

Tel: 0845 300 8090 (24/7)

www.mariestopes.org.uk

The Sexual Health Line is a free and confidential telephone service giving information and advice on HIV, AIDS and other STIs, and locating local sexual health clinics and other services. They also run a website for the under-twenty-fives called Worth Talking About, which provides information on sexual health, pregnancy and contraceptives.

Tel: 0800 567 123 (24/7)

www.nhs.uk/worthtalkingabout

The Terrence Higgins Trust is a charity that provides free emotional, legal, benefits and medical advice for those with the HIV virus and their families.

THT Direct: 0808 802 1221 (Monday-Friday 10am-10pm; Saturday-Sunday 12noon-6pm)

www.tht.org.uk

Index

piccadillypress.co.uk/teen

Go online to discover:

☆ more books you'll love

☆ competitions

☆ sneak peeks inside books

☆ fun activities, trailers and downloads

☆ author interviews

☆ and much more!